The Least Restrictive Alternative: Principles and Practices

by
H. Rutherford Turnbull, III, *Editor*
James W. Ellis
Elizabeth M. Boggs
Penelope O. Brooks
Douglas P. Biklen

Task Force on Least Restriction
Legislative and Social Issues Committee
American Association on Mental Deficiency, Inc.
5101 Wisconsin Avenue, NW, Washington, DC 20016

ISBN 0-940898-06-3
LC 81-68988
© 1981 by
American Association on Mental Deficiency, Inc.
5101 Wisconsin Avenue, N.W., Washington, D.C. 20016

Printed in the United States of America

TABLE OF CONTENTS

PREFACE

This special publication of the American Association on Mental Deficiency (AAMD) is the product of the dedication and talents of many people. It is appropriate to identify them and their roles.

More than the other contributors, James W. Ellis, presently chairman of the Legislative and Social Issues Committee (LASI) and Associate Professor of Law at the University of New Mexico, and I are responsible for the segment of the publication that deals with the legal basis for the Least Restrictive Alternative (LRA).

Elizabeth M. Boggs, an AAMD special awards recipient, former member of the LASI Committee and, like Ellis and myself, a contributor to the *Consent Handbook*, is principally responsible for some of the early schematic representations and the accompanying discussions. She also worked in conjunction with Dr. Brooks on the portion that discusses the application of LRA to mentally retarded persons and mental retardation professionals.

Penelope O. Brooks, Professor of Psychology at Peabody College, Vanderbilt University, and a former member of the LASI Committee, contributed the part that relates LRA to issues of developmental psychology and the discussion of freedom and choice therein. She also collaborated closely with Dr. Boggs on the "application" section.

Douglas P. Biklen, Director of the Center on Human Policy at Syracuse University and a former LASI member, is primarily responsible for the hypothetical examples and the discussion of LRA in the context of service-delivery systems.

The five of us have vigorously criticized each other's work, contributing both substantive and stylistic changes. We have not all been of the same mind about the principle of LRA, its uses, or its implications. Happily, we agreed to submerge our strongly held personal views so we could produce a thoughtful document about a controversial concept. For at least these reasons, it is incorrect to attribute all or any portion of this publication to any one of us individually.

Moreover, we are not the only contributors, simply the people who have become responsible for the present form of concept papers submitted by other members of the LRA Task Force: David Rosen, Gerald Provencal and David Evans, all once of the Macomb-Oakland Center, Mt. Clemens, Michigan; Benjamin Goldberg, M.D., Director of Treatment, Training and Research, CPRI, London, Ontario; Clif-

1

ford J. Drew, Professor of Special Education, University of Utah; Nancy K. Klein, Professor of Special Education, Cleveland State University; Daniel E. Smith, Coordinator of Institutional Research and Training, Parsons State Hospital, Parsons, Kansas; and Philip Roos, Executive Director, Association for Retarded Citizens and formerly Chairman of the Planning Committee of the AAMD.

In addition Ivy P. Mooring, Miles B. Santamour, James Q. Simmons and Joseph T. Weingold participated in early discussions with us about LRA.

Dennis W. Brezina of the AAMD Staff reviewed the manuscript and made necessary editorial changes.

Some people might take the position that the LRA principle should not be the subject of an Association publication until empirical research substantiates or refutes it. Others might criticize this publication itself on the grounds that it does not sufficiently refer to such empirical evidence as might exist.

The editors would reply by saying that their charge from the Association's Council was to produce a special publication that thoughtfully addresses the legal basis for the LRA principle and some of the implications of that basis. Accordingly, the publication is not intended to be empirically referenced. It is hoped that it fulfills its purpose and responsibly discharges the Council's mandate.

H. Rutherford Turnbull, III
Chairman, Task Force on Least Restriction
Chairman, Department of Special Education
University of Kansas
Secretary-Treasurer AAMD

CHAPTER I

INTRODUCTION AND STATEMENT OF CONCEPTS

A. The Task Force on Least Restriction

An important function of the American Association on Mental Deficiency has been to participate vigorously in developing concepts and advocating programs that positively affect the lives of persons who are identified as mentally retarded and professionals who provide specialized services to them. In the past several years, the Association, acting principally through its Legislative and Social Issues Committee, has been particularly active in this regard, issuing policy statements that set out its positions on rights of mentally retarded persons, moving more forcefully to influence national legislation and administrative activities that concern them, and refining such frequently-used but ill-defined notions as "consent."[1]

A natural extension of this activity is the Task Force on Least Restriction. Organized in 1976, the Task Force was charged by the Association's Council with delineating for the Association's diverse membership the various implications of the newly translated principle that mentally retarded persons should be dealt with in the way that least restricts them, i.e., "LRA" or "the LRA principle." The Council agreed that the Task Force's activity should be undertaken because the Association's policy statements referred to LRA in a variety of contexts[2] and because it appeared necessary to clarify the principle so that it might be better understood and applied by mental retardation professionals and other policy makers and administrators beyond the judicial context in which it had originally been involved.

The Task Force began its work by asking its members, who represented a wide range of professional disciplines and interests, to prepare thoughtful and provocative "concept papers" about how LRA operates in their respective domains. It then edited and integrated the concept papers into what it hopes is a logical and instructive whole.

The purpose of the resulting document, published (like the *Consent Handbook*) as a Special Publication of the Association, is to discuss LRA in the context of other principles that dramatically affect mentally retarded persons' lives and mental retardation professionals' activities. They include, among others, "normalization,"[3] "individ-

3

ualization," "equal protection," "due process," "right to choose," "right to treatment," and "right to refuse treatment." More important, however, they include principles that undergird even these highly generalized ones, namely "freedom" or "liberty," "fundamental rights" and comparative degrees of restriction. It is not possible to isolate LRA from these related principles. At the same time, LRA demands separate treatment, because its origins, conceptual structure, application to the lives of mentally retarded persons and use in developing systems to serve them are complex.

Moreover, the LRA principle is entirely consonant with those related principles, and, like them, will take on nuances and shadings that are required by, among other things, shifting notions about the meaning of the related principles, changing technology with which to assist retarded persons, reorganized service systems and successful or unsuccessful assertions of retarded persons' legal rights or claims.

This Special Publication begins by illustrating how the LRA principle arises in a variety of situations affecting mentally retarded persons' lives. It then discusses the basic concepts of "freedom" and "liberty" and shows how they relate to LRA. Next, it discusses LRA as a legal prescription, focusing on its development and application and applying LRA to mentally retarded persons in a host of contexts. It then demonstrates how LRA works in shaping the governmental systems that are designed to serve mentally retarded persons. Finally, it restates and interprets LRA as a guiding principle of professional behavior, demonstrates its relationship to the related principles and illustrates the need for professional judgment in applying LRA in individual cases. Like the *Consent Handbook*, this writing is not a prescription or cookbook. Instead, it lays out the dilemmas and issues within which LRA may be involved and offers criteria for decision making.

B. Introduction to the LRA Principle

It seems difficult, if not impossible, to escape the LRA principle. It keeps cropping up both in expected and unexpected circumstances. Consider, for example, the following hypothetical cases.

Example 1. On March 15, 1981, Frank and Martha Holland entered the Board of Education conference room at Central School District to act as witnesses in an impartial hearing convened at their request. The hearing marked a new stage in a dispute that had been brewing for several months between District officials and the parents. Ethan, their son, was classified as severely retarded. For the first three years of his school life, he attended special education and resource classes at the local Central Elementary School. But, in January, an interdisciplinary evaluation team decided that Ethan could be served "more appropriately" at the Milo School for moderately and severely retarded children.

The Hollands had only one complaint with Milo's educational offerings. They insisted that their son receive his special education in a regular school where he might have some interaction—even limited interaction—with non-disabled children. They based their claim on the language of the Federal Regulations implementing Public Law 94-142, the Education for All Handicapped Children Act, which states:

> [T]o the maximum extent appropriate, handicapped children, including children in public or private institutions or other care facilities, [shall be] educated with children who are not handicapped.[4]

The Hollands reasoned that since other school districts in the country were educating children with similarly severe disabilities in regular school settings, albeit with special education services, this should prove their claim that Ethan's least restrictive setting would be a special class in a regular school. School officials, on the other hand, argued that there was no evidence that Ethan could benefit from proximity to non-disabled children.

Who is right? Just how should the LRA doctrine be applied? If Ethan's parents were to win their case, would this spell the end of all Milo-type schools? Would all of the children with moderate and severe disabilities henceforth be served in special programs located in regular school settings? And if that were the implication, could it not be argued that in establishing the regular school as the "least restrictive" setting for Ethan, Milo School would be eliminated as a program option for many other disabled children, thereby restricting their range of options? On the other hand, if the District prevails and Ethan is kept in a segregated school, would he not be "restricted" from interacting with non-handicapped children? What does "restriction" mean, and what is "most" or "least" restrictive? Of whom? And how?

Example 2. Another case involved Tanya Hyde, a third grade student in a regular classroom of thirty at Southwestern Elementary School. One day, Tanya arrived home in tears. She explained to her mother that her teacher was recommending her for the "new room." The "new room" was a euphemism for a resource room where children receive special education instruction for part of each school day. Tanya envisioned the indignity of being called "retard," a term that "new class" kids were often called by other students. When Tanya's mother and school officials met to discuss the proposed change, battle lines formed almost immediately. School personnel, including the school psychologist, recommended the resource program. Mrs. Hyde insisted that such help, if it was necessary, be provided in Tanya's current placement. Both the school officials and Mrs. Hyde rested their positions upon the LRA concept.

As in the case of Ethan Holland, a critical problem is created when parents and professionals are on opposite sides of an issue. One or both sides were claiming that the LRA principle supported their position. Also, the controversy surrounding resolution of the issue sparked an outpouring of related questions: Should the LRA principle be weighed against competing issues, such as efficiency and economy? Should parents or professionals have the final say in these disputes? Should all people with similar classifications have LRA determined for them in the same fashion? Would implementation of LRA lead to more or less choice for the consumer? What scientific evidence exists to support application of LRA? What is "restrictive" about a special education classroom placement? What is beneficial about it? From whose point of view? Is the "least restrictive" placement always the most appropriate one?

Example 3. The parents of a profoundly retarded 12-year-old girl wanted their daughter sterilized. The parents argued that the girl could not be expected to take contraceptive pills or manage other birth control methods and that she would never be able to cope with pregnancy. But apparently of even greater concern to the mental retardation professionals who worked with the girl was the common assessment that menstruation would compound the difficulties of her already difficult life. Therefore they proposed that sterilization be accomplished by hysterectomy. Other mental retardation professionals opposed the sterilization on the grounds

6

that the girl could not consent for herself, that less intrusive (less restrictive) means of birth control should be tried, and that the benefits gained from sterilization did not warrant such an intrusive step, whether by the state or by a family and its professional advisors.

The opponents of sterilization argued that LRA requires that this drastic step should at least be postponed until alternatives can be explored. The proponents argued that LRA should not be interpreted to require that the girl become pregnant through likely failure with other methods of contraception or face sexual segregation. They also contended that preventing menstruation will give her greater liberty. Which is the proper interpretation of LRA in this case?

Example 4. For many years, a small number (about 30) of residents of a large state residential center for mentally retarded persons (population 800) have engaged in a significant amount of self-injurious behavior (SIB). There are adults and children, all severely or profoundly retarded. Each has a long history of SIB, hospitalization for treatment, release from hospital care and return to residential units, and recurring SIB. In all cases, the SIB can cause permanent and serious damage to the resident. In some cases, it could result in maiming or injury just short of death. Under the clients' current habilitation plans, only sporadic programming to reduce SIB occurs, and much of it is ineffective.

A team of psychologists, physicians, nurses, health care technicians and social workers proposed to begin a program that calls for twenty-four-hour intensive intervention for control and reduction of SIB. The program requires all the SIB residents to live in the same building until their SIB is remediated or reduced, at which time they will return to their regular living units. It also requires continuous supervision and programming by specially trained staff and the use of behavioral, pharmacological, and aversive stimuli, including electroshock devices.

The team met with the center's human rights committee for discussion and clearance of the program. Committee members raised a number of questions, including whether the possibly lengthy placement of the residents in a closely supervised program in a separate building was overly restrictive and whether the proposed interventions could not be performed without a special placement. Others responded by suggesting that the proposed

7

behavioral interventions—including positive and negative reinforcement, physical restraint, seclusion, and time-out—were always less restrictive than pharmacological interventions, because medication produced long-lasting side effects, which they called a "chemical strait jacket." Still others argued that aversive interventions allow the patient periods of·inter-shock normality which would eventually become longer. In the absence of consensus about what would be the least restrictive alternative, the program was abandoned and the residents remained in their regular living units where the staff to resident ratio was lower than in the proposed program, staff competencies were more doubtful, and SIB was dealt with only on an ad hoc basis. Was this result required by LRA?

Example 5. A new state director of mental retardation services faced a number of competing claims—all of which are defended as logical developments of the LRA principle.

The director's predecessor had begun an aggressive and controversial program of deinstitutionalization. He had placed a freeze on all new admissions to institutions, and had begun to discharge large numbers of residents. "I simply will not have any more new admissions to any of our state centers, and I will reduce the institutional population by a third within twelve months. We will place residents in less restrictive alternatives and, at the same time, save the state millions of dollars." He then began discharging adults of all ages into nursing homes.

Two lawsuits were filed against the state. The first was brought by parents of children who were on institutional waiting lists for admission. They claimed that by denying their children the option of institutional placement, the state had restricted parental choice. They also claimed that institutional programs are the optimal choice for some children, and, therefore, for those children, there is no less restrictive alternative.

The second suit was brought by the state's Protection and Advocacy Program challenging the wholesale depopulation of the institutions. This lawsuit alleged that nursing homes could not provide the kind of habilitation which mentally retarded adults needed, and called these facilities "the new back wards," where patients were relegated to conditions which had led to right to treatment suits in institutions. The complaint concluded that this particular type of deinstitutionalization was moving clients into facilities which were more restrictive than institutions, even though they were smaller and located in the community.

In the face of these lawsuits and the accompanying bad publicity, the previous director had resigned. In addition to the litigation, the new director faced various political pressures. The nursing home operators claimed he cannot reverse the policy of his predecessor. They noted that they have made large expansion investments in relying on the policy and claimed that their clients were better off away from the restrictions of institutions. The chairperson of the state Senate Finance Committee strongly "suggested" that the policy be retained because budgetary savings were beginning to result from the program, and argued that problems of restrictive conditions can be remedied by tighter inspection and licensing requirements. Finally, another group of parents and professionals urged the new director to continue deinstitutionalization, but only as new high-quality alternatives, which, incidentally, are more expensive than nursing homes, are set up in the community.

In this example, every interest group uses a version of LRA to support their position. To what extent are the policy choices faced by the new director governed by principles of relative restrictiveness? Is client mobility the relevant restriction? The client's distance from his own community? His freedom to associate with persons unlike himself? The kinds of choices which he may make or which may be made for him? And how does the quality and appropriateness of care fit into a debate argued in terms of LRA rhetoric?

It should be obvious from these hypothetical cases that it is not simple to identify situations to which LRA applies, much less to apply the principle to the situation itself. Essentially, LRA is an important principle because it occupies a pivotal role in professional and governmental decisions concerning the treatment of persons who are retarded, and yet it is inseparable from basic concepts of "freedom" and "liberty."

C. "Freedom" and "Liberty" and "More" and "Less": The Concepts in Conjunction with which a Concept of "Least Restriction" is Developed

A discussion of "restriction" that does not mention the "freedom" and "liberty" that may be subject to restriction does not advance the analysis of LRA. Similarly, it is not instructive to discuss "least restriction'' without discussing the factors which make an option "more" or "less" restrictive. Unhappily, the literature on "least restriction," almost without exception, discusses LRA without also analyzing "freedom," "liberty," or what is meant by degrees of restriction.

In the third century of this Republic, Americans still cherish freedom and liberty, both the specific guarantees of the Bill of Rights and the general liberties to be free from undue government interference in the disposition of one's time, attention and resources in the choice of associates, place of residence and employment, and the like. Closely associated with these freedoms are the traditional right and duty of parents to control the care and upbringing of their children and the right of obligation of professionals who serve these people to act with discretion in what they perceive to be the best interest of their clients.

In fact, however, nobody is entirely free; each of us operates under many constraints, some quite severe. These constraints are physical, social, legal, economic and moral or ethical. Constraints are inevitable because, on a planet of finite size, the choices open to one individual affect the choices open to other individuals (no two people being free to choose to occupy the same space at the same time or to consume the same resources). One man's privacy may preclude another's access, one woman's freedom of speech may require others to listen. Freedom is relative, subject to change as people and conditions change, and dependent upon the existence of conditions in which it may be exercised.

It is useful to examine these constraints according to a two-dimensional schema (Table 1) that recognizes that while some constraints are "natural," others are imposed by society. Certain are imposed on all or at least many citizens while others are imposed only on individuals who are individually identified for extraordinary treatment, i.e., restriction. The schema also recognizes that certain restrictions are more restrictive than others. For example, a traumatic double amputee who cannot feed himself is more restrained than a person who imposes certain moral choices on himself, e.g., partial fasting, and who can later choose to lift those moral constraints. Similarly, certain restrictions are less restricting than others. Imprisonment restricts not only a person's right to drive (as do drivers' license laws regarding persons who suffer uncontrollable seizures) but also the person's right to walk freely in society. Finally,

10

TABLE 1

Typology of constraints by source and object, with examples.

Object of Constraint / Source of Constraint	(general application) ALL Persons (usual)	(wide but not universal application) Members of Defined GROUPS (frequent)	(selective application) INDIVIDUAL (extraordinary, unique)
Natural	inability to fly	some persons are infertile	traumatic double amputee can't feed self
Moral (self regulated)	compulsion to act for self preservation	parental sense of duty to protect offspring	individual ethical/ moral decision; "obedience to the unenforceable," e.g., vow of celibacy
Societal	respect for private property/traffic rules/professional duties to clients (e.g., Canons of Ethics)	compulsory education of children; military duty	imprisonment; person with uncontrolled seizures may not drive; mentally disabled alien may not immigrate

the schema recognizes that restrictions can be imposed by governments, by professionals acting under legally sanctioned authority and by the restricted individuals themselves as a matter of personal choice.

The schema does not represent the value that Americans put upon their freedom, which is only hinted at above and bears more than a brief mention.

What is freedom? How much of it does anyone have? Liberty was defined by the Supreme Court in 1923 thus: "[It] denotes not merely freedom from bodily restraint, but also the right of the individual to contract, to engage in any of the common occupations of life, to acquire useful knowledge, to marry, establish a home and bring up children, to worship God according to the dictates of his own conscience, and generally, to enjoy those privileges long recognized in common law as essential to the orderly pursuit of happiness by free men."[5]

Because the Constitution was framed by men who saw freedom as a God-given right, no one should argue with the belief that any law-abiding American should be allowed to live as freely as he desires at any given time. The Constitution, however, permits the government, upon a sufficient showing of necessity, to curtail the freedom enjoyed by any of its citizens. Thus, a person who is dangerous to others may be involuntarily committed. Likewise, a person may not be free to burn leaves in his or her garden, default on his taxes, or abandon his minor child. These legal prohibitions are imposed in the communal interest to protect the rights of others, prevent harm to others and promote the general welfare. The nature of society's interest in each case may vary, for example, communal interests include, respectively, public safety, public health and environmental safety, public fiscal stability and financing of public services, and the protection of especially vulnerable people. As the schema indicates, there are numerous other constraints on freedom such as cultural or moral, fiscal and physical.

Education is a major field in which individual liberties are curtailed in the public interest. Along with the right to education, the law of most states imposes a duty to be educated. It is understandably in the public interest that children be restrained from choosing to grow up functionally illiterate and vocationally incompetent. In fact, a combination of tradition and a need to address both equity and efficiency has converted mandatory schooling into a highly structured system in which rules and procedures limit educators' and students' ranges of choices. Recent legislation and litigation implementing handicapped students' right to education have added more procedures and regulations.[6] Even children without special problems have little latitude to choose a particular school, a particular class or, in the early grades at least, an individualized curriculum. It was once thought that excluding handicapped children from school freed them from the "restriction" of schooling, which, it was presumed, would not benefit them. This is no longer the case, reflecting a changing set of principles applicable to the education of all children and entailing new accommodations to cultural diversity and new concepts of the appropriate roles for public schools.

Conversely, as the changes enforced in public schools well demonstrate, any newly enunciated right for one person or group places a new responsibility and hence constraint on the freedom of others. Freedom is not limitless. The best one can hope to do is to maximize it within a reasonably equitable system. This is the issue of "competing equities."[7] Hence, we have laws that restrict individuals' freedom and a federal Constitution that pursues "equity" through the equal protection clause.

D. How "Freedom" and "Liberty" are Restricted: The Means by which Choices by Mentally Retarded Persons or Mental Retardation Professionals are Limited and the Doctrines that Guide and Shape Decisions about these Limitations

In the *Consent Handbook*, the Association's Task Force on Consent dealt, in large part, with the legal and professional techniques available for increasing or maximizing one kind of freedom—the individual choice that mentally retarded persons or their representatives and mental retardation professionals have over decisions affecting the lives of those who are mentally retarded.

The obverse of that focus is on how freedom, i.e., choice, is limited. In current legal and mental retardation terminology, much attention is focused on "restriction," i.e., the means that may be used to limit individual choice (whether of retarded persons or of their representatives and mental retardation professionals), and the doctrines, both legal and other, that may be used to guide and shape those limitations. As indicated above, limitations are necessarily inherent in the notion of freedom, which is, after all, a relative concept.

Aside from the limits set by fair play ("equity"), there are at least two other reasons for limiting individual choice. The first and most frequent motivation for the limitation is social cost. We cannot afford to make all conceivable options available to every individual. We employ value judgments about individual and social utility in choosing which options to make available in a given situation. Some options are "better" than others, so only those options are available within the permissible range which individual election permits. This function is not merely related to the economics of keeping a manageable number of choices open; it is also frequently a substantive judgment that, even though an additional choice would not make the number of options unmanageable, the additional option is so "bad" (worthless, harmful, costly, or whatever) that it should be excluded from the range of options on its own merits.

Secondly, individual choice is limited because human beings can tolerate only so many choices with any degree of comfort or personal efficiency. Frequently this is a serendipitous consequence rather than a motivation for limitation. For example, a restaurant menu can be so vast as to discourage the diner.

Various people or agencies impose limitations on choice. Parents limit their children. The most obvious legal limitations are created by direct governmental action—restrictions, mandatory procedures, etc. A government operates somewhat less visibly (and possibly less accountably) but no less effectively when it decides what types of health care to finance for the indigent (e.g., Medicaid coverage for most surgery) or what services it chooses to finance for that larger public group which relies upon such governmentally funded services as public schools.

But governments are not the only agencies that limit choice to mentally retarded people. Families and professionals also shape and thereby limit the range of choices available to the retarded individual. The role of professionals is particularly important. The decisions about their own services, the recommendations they make to clients and the manner in which they convey those recommendations serve to enhance or limit a retarded person's choice, in fact, even if not in law.

Professionals make decisions limiting the choices of others similarly to, and sometimes reflecting, the manner in which governments including courts, accomplish the same task. It is therefore appropriate to show how governments limit the range of individual choice.

A government may accomplish a limitation in any of three ways. The first is to create an irrebuttable presumption, i.e., a decision not to make a certain option available in any case, irrespective of individual factors. An example is a rule that no minor may be legally sterilized. The law maker might admit in a moment of candor that there are extremely mature minors who would be as capable of giving consent as effectively as the average adult (to whom the irrebuttable presumption does not apply). But this method of limitation is chosen because (1) it is thought that few minors fall within this category; (2) it is difficult to determine accurately that judgments made by or for a given minor will prove appropriate later in life; and (3) it is felt that there is little disadvantage in postponing a decision until the individual reaches majority.

The rule-making body decides, therefore, to accept a less-than-perfect decision in a small minority of cases rather than risk individual case-by-case determinations that may produce a larger number of results that are "bad," "worse," or too costly to society.

14

Another method by which government can limit individual choice is by making a determination in each case, ungoverned and uninfluenced by preconceived notions of what is probably the correct result. The advantage of this model of decision-making is that it creates no bad results. (Like everything else, it can produce bad results because of fallible individual judgments). The disadvantages are the high cost of individual scrutiny in each case and the creation of irreconcilable results—rules cannot be easily deduced from such decision making, providing scant guidance for individuals wishing to conform voluntarily to the results accomplished by governmental decisions.

A middle ground exists between irrebuttable presumptions and a system of unguided case-by-case analysis. Frequently governments impose limitations on the basis of a rebuttable presumption. In these situations, the government establishes a prescriptive generalization that one set of options, or one end of a spectrum of options, is preferred over other alternatives. A showing of extraordinary circumstances will have to occur if the "less preferred" option is to be implemented. This model has greater flexibility than the irrebuttable presumption and greater regularity, predictability, and avoidance of a preceived potential for abuse or harm than the unguided case-by-case method. A system of rebuttable presumptions allows greater freedom of choice than the first model. The individual can find his way into the "exceptional" class if he or she can make the required showing. This allows the government to skew the decisionmaking process away from a "less desirable" alternative with decisions clustering around the option which has been predetermined to be preferred.

The awarding of child custody upon the divorce of the parents is an example that may clarify the operation of these three models. The law has traditionally reflected a societal judgment that children should be with their mother if they could not remain in an intact family. One method of accomplishing this would be to make an irrebuttable presumption that, where parents contested custody, preference would always be given to the mother. But it was clear, particularly in the era of fault-based divorce, that when litigants had incentive to bring out undesirable aspects of each other's character, the mother was not always capable of exercising her parental responsibilities. So the law has operated under a system of rebuttable presumptions. The mother would be awarded custody unless the court was convinced that she was an unfit parent, in which case custody would be awarded to the father or to another person. In operation, this system meant that most children of divorced families ended up living with their mothers, but in a minority of exceptional cases, where this posed a threat to their well-being, they could live with their fathers. A change in attitudes about sex roles has weakened the assumption that children are better off with their mothers. In some jurisdictions this has led to a change in the presumption of maternal custody.

One way to reflect this change is to abandon the system of rebuttable presumptions and replace it with a case-by-case determination of which is the more appropriate custodial parent unguided by any presumption about sex. Another way is to change the barrier for overcoming the presumption. Previously the father had to show that the mother was an unfit parent. That barrier could be lowered so that the father is required to show only that he is a better parent than the mother. This is a lower barrier because the mother might not meet the absolute standard of "unfit" but might fail in comparison with her ex-husband. Which option is selected will largely determine how many fathers receive custody of their children because a judge may continue to use the old rebuttable presumption measure in fact while purporting to apply the newer standard. He or she may prefer to draw informal guidance from a rule that had guided him or her formally in the past. This highlights the previous point about the discomfort of too many choices.

Take an example from the area of mental retardation. Regarding guardianship, it was presumed that once an adult is shown to be incompetent, he or she is incompetent for all purposes and his or her guardian accordingly could exercise plenary control over him or her. In many states, this is still the law. In those states the law maker (government) has created an irrebuttable presumption: Once adjudged incompetent, an individual is fully incompetent. Though true for some mentally retarded persons, it certainly is not true for all. Limited competence—indeed, even situational competence— coexists with limited guardianship law.[8] In the states that have adopted limited guardianship law, the law maker is moving from an irrebuttable to a rebuttable presumption of total incompetence following an adjudication. The incompetent may be shown to have residual competence, and, in those areas of competence, he or she retains control, i.e., choice, over his or her actions, and the guardian is legally barred from acting on his or her behalf.

Take another example. Until not too long ago, some states adhered to an antediluvian practice of requiring mentally retarded persons to

16

be sterilized before they were discharged from state institutions. The presumptions behind this practice were based on the interest of preventing propagation of "unfit" people, on the interest of future children in not having a retarded parent and on the state in not having to support the offspring of retarded parents through welfare assistance. As in the case with guardianship, the presumption was irrebuttable: no discharge without sterilization.

The LRA doctrine fits neatly into the middle of these models of governmental, personal, family, and professional decisionmaking. LRA takes on the role of a rebuttable presumption. First, the government (or person, family, or professional) presumes that there is a generally accepted hierarchy of placements, treatments, or interventions and that any given one is clearly rank ordered as more or less restrictive. The "more restrictive" is posited to be the less desirable as a matter of social policy, law, and habilitation. Second, the presumption can be overcome in an individual case only upon a showing of necessity to accomplish a valid state purpose or a greater appropriateness for the benefit of the individual.

For example, the presumption in favor of an individual's liberty can be overcome and a valid state purpose also can be accomplished if the person is adjudicated dangerous to himself or others because of his mental disability. In cases of involuntary commitment, the individual has been found to be dangerous and therefore the state's interest in public safety overcomes the presumption and the individual may be temporarily deprived of his liberty. This is the classic case.

Given that *some* restriction is justifiable, LRA must also be applied to the nature of the solution, in this case the commitment itself. LRA enters the picture here through the presumption that the commitment cannot be more restrictive than necessary to accomplish the state's purpose. Therefore, if it can be shown that a particular placement, e.g., in solitary confinement or "isolation," is not necessary to meet a retarded person's habilitation needs or to protect society from dangerous behavior, LRA will support arguments that the individual should receive services in a less restrictive setting, e.g., in an "open" ward or in the "community" under supervision. Many of the recent LRA court cases frontally attack the placement of retarded persons in institutional settings as being excessively restrictive particularly when compared to community alternatives.[9]

The presumption against restriction can also be rebutted by showing that a particular treatment is appropriate for the benefit of the individual. Behavioral intervention is, by definition, restrictive, in the same ways that compulsory education is. Yet, it may be argued (rebutted) that such restriction, in the long run, results in a less dependent individual.

Even decisions regarding which behavioral treatment to impose on a client are subject to interpretation within this framework. Certain courts, legislatures, executive agencies and professionals allow only positive reinforcements to be used in behavior modification programs. This policy could be considered a rebuttable presumption. Negative contingencies are allowed only after positive ones do not succeed in producing the desired result.[10] The presumption can be overcome if the negative consequences are less restrictive.

These examples demonstrate two points made earlier. First, total freedom is both unacceptable and impossible to obtain. Second, governments and individuals, including mental retardation professionals, respond to this by establishing standards that accommodate the constitutional, personal and professional rights of liberty with competing rights of protection or habilitation. Governments do it through the legal use of presumptions. Individuals do it by making assumptions, creating and following commonly accepted conventions and protocols or choosing to limit and restrict their activities. Whether as legal presumptions or nonlegal assumptions, these accommodations are powerful and pervasive. Everyone—lawmaker, professional and client—has a role in limiting his or her own and the other's freedom.

One concern in analyzing the LRA doctrine is with the lives of persons who are subject to the natural limitations imposed by retardation. Another concern centers on limitations that lawmakers either impose on professionals or that professionals impose on themselves, which in turn are imposed on mentally retarded persons. In a nutshell, do these presumptions and assumptions, part and parcel of the LRA concept, overly restrict mentally retarded persons? Do governments and professionals misunderstand and misapply the LRA doctrine so that it becomes a force for further limitation? As in the *Consent Handbook,* the editors' preference is to increase the range of choice for retarded people and mental retardation professionals by infusing the LRA doctrine with a sense of liberation, not a sense of restriction.

Two important points must be made before proceeding. The first involves reconciling competing values. Both consent requirements and the LRA principle are based upon the value of human freedom, but their practical implementation, as the examples have indicated, may place these two doctrines in conflict. The resolution of such conflicts is neither clear nor easy. A single-minded focus on the ideology of LRA may unacceptably reduce individual choice by eliminating valuable options. Thus the LRA doctrine, which is valued because it is a tool for enhancing human freedom, may unacceptably infringe upon freedom of choice. Similarly, single-minded focus on consent, to the exclusion of LRA, may prevent the development of a client's *capacity* for choice by keeping a client in a setting in which he or she cannot develop his or her independence and abilities. A refusal, in the name of free choice, to eliminate or limit restrictive alternatives may inhibit the development of less restrictive alternatives which could better serve many clients.

The second point involves the utility and desirability of the LRA doctrine. The authors of this book will have occasion to criticize applications of the doctrine because those applications may reduce the choices open to mentally retarded people in a detrimental way. The editors acknowledge differences among ourselves about which applications of LRA are justified and which are more or less beneficial in the lives of retarded people. But we remain firm and unanimous in our belief that LRA is an important legal doctrine which has and will be used to enhance the freedom of retarded people while accommodating the interests of society in its general welfare and the particular welfare of retarded citizens. When we disagree with some past applications of LRA (and when we have disagreed with one another) it has been within the context of these shared beliefs.

Having first shown the relationship of LRA to freedom, liberty, and degrees of restriction and choice, having illustrated how it is used by governments and professionals as a technique for making decisions about mentally retarded persons, and having shown some of the risks arising from a misunderstanding of LRA as a decision-making technique, it will be useful to examine LRA's legal history and professional uses in more detail.

CHAPTER II

LRA AS A PRINCIPLE OF LAW

A. "Equal Protection," Substantive Due Process," and "Procedural Due Process": Basic Legal Concepts

Just as it is futile to discuss "least restriction" without first analyzing "freedom," "liberty," and "degrees of restriction," so it is difficult to understand the legal significance of "least restriction" without first understanding the basic legal concepts out of which the LRA legal principle has developed.[11] There are three main concepts. Each is drawn from the Fourteenth Amendment's limitation on state power: "No State shall . . . deprive any person of life, liberty, or property, without due process of law; nor deny to any person within its jurisdiction the equal protection of the laws." (The same limitations are extended to the Federal government's actions by the Fifth Amendment).

Procedural due process refers to the requirement that before the government deprives an individual of "life, liberty, or property," it must provide him or her with a hearing or procedure to determine the necessity or appropriateness of the deprivation. The core of this requirement is fairness, and the methods used to achieve this fairness are individualization and accountability. Before the State can deprive a person of liberty (one of the most frequent issues for mentally retarded people), it must show that the deprivation is warranted by the facts of that person's individual case. The individual must be given an opportunity to protest the proposed action. The right to protest, i.e., the right to be heard, carries with it certain procedural safeguards designed to assure fairness. A familiar example of procedural due process is the criminal justice system. Persons accused of crimes, from minor offenses to the most heinous, have the right to a trial, to an impartial decision-maker (judge or jury), to assistance of counsel, to confront and cross-examine opposing witnesses, and to present witnesses in their own defense. These requirements are drawn from society's notions of fundamental fairness and from specific constitutional guarantees.

But since government can deprive people, including retarded people, of their liberty by means other than criminal prosecution, courts have had to face the question of "what process is due" in the case of noncriminal deprivations. An obvious example is civil commitment of mentally ill or mentally retarded people.[12] Also important is the exclusion of handicapped children from public schools,[13] or the placement of a child in an arguably stigmatizing special education program or category.[14] Similarly, the exclusion of retarded people from any service or benefit program may raise procedural due process issues.

The United States Supreme Court has developed a balancing test for determining "what process is due" in cases outside the criminal justice system. Under this test, the nature of the private interest involved (physical liberty, freedom from stigmatization or whatever) is weighed against the likelihood of erroneous decisions being made without procedural protections. For example, would persons be incorrectly placed in institutions if no hearings were held? Also weighed is the likelihood that procedural protections would cure some of those errors against the state's interest in avoiding the protections, e.g., the financial cost of providing hearings.[15] Boiled down to its essentials, this test means that if an important interest is involved in a person's life, and if he or she can show that a mistake may be made without the opportunity for a hearing, a hearing must be provided.[16] Readers of the *Consent Handbook* will recall a parallel. Consent procedures are expected to be more elaborate when the outcome is riskier, more intrusive, or less reversible.

Procedural due process is related to LRA because the due process hearing will be the forum for a retarded person or his advocate to point out a less restrictive or less drastic means of accomplishing the State's goals. Thus the individual can force the government to demonstrate why the rebuttable presumption of every person's liberty should be set aside under the facts of this particular case. The individualization and accountability provided by the availability of hearings are a major protection of individual freedoms.

Substantive due process, while drawn from the same clause in ths Constitution, has a quite different meaning. This meaning of the Due Process Clause says that the state simply cannot do something regardless of whether it provides elaborate procedural protections and hearings. While procedural due process is grounded in fairness to the individual, substantive due process places outer limits on what the government can do. Thus, certain kinds of governmental deprivation of liberty are simply impermissible.

A now familiar example of substantive due process is the constituted right of a woman, as affirmed by the Supreme Court in 1973,

22

to be free from any state-imposed barrier to her choice to seek an abortion performed by a qualified practitioner during the first or second trimester of pregnancy.[17] That is, the state does not have the option of denying her the right to an abortion merely by providing her with a due process hearing. It simply cannot interfere with this aspect of her right to privacy.

A recent mental health case is closely analogous to the field of mental retardation. In *O'Connor v. Donaldson,*[18] the Supreme Court unanimously ruled that a State may not confine a non-dangerous person in a mental hospital in mere custodial confinement. The state might be able to confine him in an institution if it gave him an adequate hearing (procedural due process) *and* showed that he was dangerous to himself or to others, or possibly if it could show that he needed treatment and such treatment would be provided. But without those added findings, the state was powerless to confine him, even if it provided him with an elaborate hearing. This limit on the state's power springs from the substantive meaning of the due process clause. Other substantive due process issues in the lives of mentally retarded people might include limitations on the power of the state to deny them necessary medical care and habilitation while they are in state control. The so-called "right to treatment" cases are substantive due process cases.

The LRA doctrine developed directly from substantive due process theory. It holds that the state does not have the power to use more restrictive (drastic, intrusive, hazardous, limiting) means than are necessary to accomplish its purpose.

Equal protection requires the government to deal even-handedly with people who are similarly situated. It holds that state discrimination between groups of people or individuals must have a sufficient justification, or the state action will be struck down as unconstitutional.[19]

Since almost any state action will treat different people differently (for example, rich people are, at least theoretically, taxed at a higher rate than poor people), and since such actions cannot all be unconstitutional, the Supreme Court has devised yet another legal test for the resolution of equal protection claims. In most cases, the state action will be upheld if it can be shown that the state had a rational reason for treating the groups differently. This is usually a very easy test for the state to meet. For example, it will have no difficulty in showing that it had a sufficient reason for taxing people at different rates when their incomes are different. But in two special categories

23

of cases, the state will have to show much more. In those categories it will have to prove that it had a compelling reason to discriminate, and the Court has held that this is such a high standard that compelling reasons are almost impossible to come by. The two categories in which the state will be hard-pressed to justify discrimination are (1) cases which involve a *classification* which the Court treats as *suspect,* such as race, and (2) cases which involve *fundamental rights,* such as the right to vote and the right to procreate.[20] When a case of discriminatory treatment involves either a suspect classification or a fundamental right or both, the Court will be quite reluctant to approve it. When neither of those factors is present, the state will have an easier time in having its action upheld as "rational."

A familiar example of equal protection was the Supreme Court's 1954 decision outlawing racial segregation in the schools.[21] Since the state action involved a suspect classification (race), the states would have had to show that they had a compelling interest in keeping the races separate in schools, and they could not do so.

Equal protection was also the basis for the right to education cases which challenged the exclusion of handicapped children from public schools.[22] While education is not a fundamental right under the federal constitution, and while the courts have never considered the question of whether mental retardation is a suspect classification, states would have a hard time showing that they had a rational basis for excluding children on the basis of their handicap. (Of course, resorting to the Constitution is no longer necessary in right to education cases, because denying education to such children is now prohibited by P.L. 94-142, by section 504 of the Vocational Rehabilitation Act, and by the laws of all states.)

Equal protection is the constitutional requirement of even-handedness on the part of the State and the prohibition against its unjustified discrimination. The relation to LRA is that various laws that have the Equal Protection Clause as their basis (e.g., P.L. 94-142) have adopted LRA as an implementing device to assure that all persons are treated fairly.

In summary, all three of the doctrines, which are derived from the Fourteenth Amendment, have a common purpose. They serve as limitations on the way in which states can deal with individuals. These protections extend to mentally retarded persons and children, just as they do to other members of society. The notion of limitations on government power is at the very heart of LRA. But the process of limiting governmental actions also unavoidably limits the actions of people, e.g., mental retardation professionals who work for the government, and, in so doing, LRA affects the options available to retarded persons and others served by government. Many limitations are undeniably beneficial, while others are more controversial. Before evaluating their effects, it is important to understand how LRA evolved from the constitutional principles described above and how it relates to the field of mental retardation.

B. LRA's Origin: The Constitutional Principle of Minimum Intrusion

The Supreme Court developed the LRA doctrine as a means of limiting what governments could do to an individual even where the Court acknowledged that the government had a legitimate interest in doing *something*.[23] Without LRA, the substantive meaning of the Due Process Clause and other constitutional provisions would present courts with rather stark alternatives. In an area of controversy, the courts could either say that the government could do anything it wanted to do or that the government could do nothing at all. Those alternatives do not allow much room for flexibility. A middle ground for judicial action was needed, and the Court devised LRA to meet that need.

An example from an early LRA case from outside the mental retardation field may help clarify the point. Arkansas once required every school teacher to file an annual affidavit listing every organization to which he or she had belonged or contributed money in the preceding five years. The State defended this requirement on the grounds of assuring the competence and fitness of its public school teachers. The Supreme Court struck down the law as unconstitutional. The Court did not deny that Arkansas had a legitimate interest in ascertaining whether its teachers were fit for their duties, but ruled that the State could (and indeed must) accomplish this legitimate end by means which intruded less drastically into the rights of the teachers. In more concrete terms, the State had a right to know whether an individual was competent to be a teacher, but it did not need to know whether he or she was a member of the NAACP in order to accomplish that end.[24]

Thus the core of LRA is one of common sense, given our preference for limited government. It states that where the government can accomplish a legitimate end in either of two ways—one which infringes individual liberty to a greater extent and another to a lesser

25

extent—the state is obligated to accomplish its goal by the less drastic means. When either a bazooka or a fly-swatter will kill the fly, preference shall be given to the fly-swatter.[25]

It is important to recognize that the LRA doctrine is only applicable, indeed, it is only needed, when the original purpose of the government is legitimate. To refer to the metaphor of the last example, LRA comes into play only when it has been determined that it is permissible to kill the fly. Therefore, LRA cannot be used by the State to get around the prohibitions of equal protection or procedural or substantive due process. If those doctrines provide that the state cannot do a particular activity, LRA will not change that judgment. But where the State is seeking to advance toward a legitimate end, LRA teaches that the State is not free to choose means which unnecessarily circumscribe individual rights.

While doctrinal sources of LRA can be found in substantive due process and in other constitutional law, more important is the *practical* incentive for the development of the doctrine. It is a method of limiting governmental intrusion into peoples' lives and rights even when the government is acting in an area which is properly open to governmental action. With LRA, courts can protect both the individual's right and the right of government to pursue its legitimate interests.[26]

C. The LRA Doctrine as Applied to Mentally Retarded Citizens

Law reformers have enlarged the rights and entitlements of mentally retarded persons and simultaneously chipped away at the restrictions imposed on them. This two-pronged strategy has been applied in the usual forums where laws are made, applied and construed—state legislatures and Congress, executive agencies of local, state and federal government, and state and federal courts. The following discussion of how LRA is applied to mentally retarded citizens will demonstrate the underlying strategy, the variety of forums in which it is advanced, and LRA's usefulness in making the strategy successful.

Involuntary Commitment. All states have statutes that authorize the courts to order persons dangerous to themselves or others committed against their will to state facilities for the mentally ill, the mentally retarded, or the criminally insane. Ostensibly, these statutes serve three distinct legitimate purposes: protecting the public from dangerous people; protecting dangerous people from themselves;

and making treatment available to people who need it but lack the ability or will to seek it.

Clearly, these statutes have not served all the purposes they purported to serve. Surely, the public was being protected from dangerous people. Not quite as surely, these dangerous people were being protected from themselves. Still less certain was that these persons were given a realistic opportunity to be habilitated while in custody. Most emphatically, involuntary commitment was being used to rid communities of undesirable people or to put into the state's hands those who seemed unable to take care of themselves and for whom nobody wanted to be responsible.

Faced with multiple and sometimes illegitimate uses of involuntary commitment statutes, lawyers set out to find familiar legal doctrines that would remedy the obvious abuses. Given that a person's liberty is at risk when an involuntary commitment hearing is held and that his liberty is denied him if he is found committable, they obviously could rely on the Fifth and Fourteenth amendments' substantive due process right of liberty.

For some clients the lawyers would be able to argue successfully that there was no need for state intervention (commitment) at all. Where the individual could be shown to be "capable of surviving safely in freedom with the assistance of willing family and friends," the state would have no compelling reason for depriving him of liberty.[27] Thus these cases could be argued on straight substantive due process grounds.

But for other clients, it could be contended that the State had a legitimate reason for intervention. These individuals were not, in fact, capable of surviving safely without some form of intervention. The question was whether the Constitution placed any limitations on what the state could do for (to) these people.[28] This is the point at which LRA enters the picture. LRA can be used in support of the argument that, even though the state is justified in intervening in this person's life, its power is neither limitless nor beyond review. Thus arguments for less drastic intervention by the state in such cases can take a number of forms. For example, a client may need out-patient therapy or other non-residential services. For a second client, it may mean that he needs assistance with life's tasks—assistance which can range from guardianship to housekeeping. A third client may require residential services, but could do as well, if not better, in a group home, rather than a large state facility.

27

Each of these alternatives would, under the proper circumstances, be less restrictive than placement in an institution. In each of these cases, LRA provides the means for enhancing the individual's freedom and for individualizing the process of selecting needed services while accommodating the state's legitimate interest and the individual's rights.

Institutional Conditions Lawsuits. LRA's accommodating function proved equally useful in litigation which challenged conditions under which people lived in state mental retardation facilities. In a number of cases in which the names are familiar to mental retardation professionals—*Wyatt,*[29] *Willowbrook,*[30] *Welsch,*[31] *Pennhurst,*[32] and others—Federal courts found institutional conditions unacceptable.

The most common means for reaching this finding has been the substantive due process theory of a *right to treatment.* States have contended that the purpose of institutions is for the provision of treatment or habilitation. But upon careful examination of the functioning of the facilities, the courts—such as the Wyatt Court—have concluded that adequate treatment or habilitation is not being provided to the residents. Through the testimony of prominent mental retardation professionals, the courts have learned about the potential for retarded people who receive individualized habilitation and have concluded that habilitation must be provided where that is the only offered justification for confining individual residents. This theory is based upon substantive due process. The state has no power to confine people for treatment without providing the treatment. Another way to look at the theory is in terms of a *quid pro quo.* The State deprives an individual of liberty for the purposes of treatment and cannot justify the continued deprivation without providing the treatment. This argument parallels that for compulsory schooling.

In the *Willowbrook* case, the court used a different method to reach the same result. It announced that mentally retarded residents had a right to *protection from harm* at the hands of the State, and, then after expert testimony, concluded that residents were being harmed by the lack of adequate habilitation.

Having made these findings, the courts were faced with the task of devising a form of relief which they could order to enforce the residents' rights. Most courts began by ordering that conditions in the institutions be brought up to constitutionally minimal standards. This entailed increasing staffing ratios, providing services that had been neglected, giving each resident an individualized habilitation plan, etc. These measures were costly, and most of the courts expressed discomfort at having to intrude so deeply into the operations of state government, but they concluded that there was no other way to protect and enhance the lives of the persons who would remain in the institutions.

In the course of the litigation, the courts also discovered that many of the residents did not require the services of a "total" institution. As a result, the courts ordered the beginning of a process that would move many or all of the residents into settings better tailored to meet their individual needs.[33] This is the point at which the judges employed the LRA doctrine. As in the civil commitment examples cited above, they concluded that many of the residents needed assistance from the state, but their needs could be met in settings less restrictive of individual liberty than in the institutions subject to the lawsuits. Thus, under the banner of LRA, courts ordered the deinstitutionalization of retarded people from large institutions into community-based programs. The doctrine provided that the state has the right and duty to provide habilitation services for these people. Even though specialized residential settings might be required, the state could not use institutional settings for clients who did not require them.

A few final observations are in order on the relationship of deinstitutionalization and LRA. Some courts have used LRA to order the dismantling of institutions. Others have used it and other doctrines to change the conditions of institutions, making them less restrictive of residents' freedom and thereby requiring additional resources for institutional care. Another judicial use of the doctrine has been to order the state to create new alternatives to institutions, alternatives that are technologically feasible but which the state had not chosen to provide.[34] Yet another use of the doctrine has been to order the transfer of individual clients into less restrictive settings.

Each of these approaches raises serious policy questions, such as the shift in decisionmaking power from the elected officials of a state to appointed federal judges. By taking basic service decisions away from the state's political arena, the courts have assured that the states cannot continue to ignore the basic human needs of some institutionalized people. But at the same time they have made it very difficult to consider the extent of those needs in the light of competing claims for state resources. Thus, judicial enforcement of these specific rights for a small number of retarded people is a short-term solution.[35]

Another problem area involves decisionmaking by law-trained judges about technical and complicated matters within the province and expertise of medical and educational professional. The use of expert testimony can do a great deal to alleviate this problem.

A related difficulty is that judicial decisions about what is "more" or "less" restrictive may introduce serious inflexibility into the service delivery system. This inflexibility may result when technologies change but the courts do not modify their orders in response to the change. Also courts' orders can only be so detailed; generalizations about restriction and about the needs of retarded people are inevitable. Restriction in the lives of retarded people is not a simple choice of "more" or "less," and the proper answer is not awaiting discovery along a simple one-dimensional spectrum of restriction. If courts use irrebuttable presumptions in the LRA orders, they may create undue problems for individuals. Fewer problems will arise if courts (and other rule-makers), while fully enforcing the LRA principle, allow for exceptional individual cases, making their presumptions rebuttable.

The final problem is one of justiciability, the ability of courts to resolve disputes effectively. Do the courts have the power to order other branches of government to spend money to create alternatives that are less restrictive than institutions? The United States Supreme Court has never directly ruled on this question, the ultimate resolution of which is in some doubt. But there is no doubt that from a number of perspectives it is preferable for states to create voluntarily a range of habilitation services that are adequate to meet the varying needs of retarded people without necessarily restricting their liberty. By such action the states will render judicial intervention unnecessary. But as long as states decline to take such action, continued controversy over judicial orders implementing LRA can be anticipated.

D. The Right to Consent and the Right to Refuse Treatment

The relationship of LRA to civil commitment and deinstitutionalization is relatively apparent, but the doctrine is also related more subtly to issues of treatment choice. It is ironic that either the LRA doctrine or its absence can serve to limit individual freedom of choice. An ever-increasing body of case law requires that adequate consent be obtained before treatment is provided to mentally handicapped people. As pointed out in the *Consent Handbook,* there is a rebuttable presumption that every individual can make his or her own decision about accepting or refusing treatment. The presumption of direct consent can be overcome by showing that the individual is incapable of making the decision for himself or herself. If the presumption is rebutted, a substitute decision-maker will be chosen to accept or refuse treatment on the individual's behalf. Whether consent is given directly or by a surrogate (such as a guardian), it must be competent, informed, and voluntary. A treatment provider who acts without obtaining legally adequate consent may be liable for damages in a lawsuit.

To the extent that the LRA principle forecloses considering options thought to be restrictive, it may work to limit the range of choices available to the individual. To the extent that LRA eliminates all options except the one predetermined to be least restrictive, it reduces the scope of individual choice to "take it or leave it." In this way, LRA may work to reduce an individual's opportunity to control his or her life, even though the purpose of the doctrine is to promote individual freedom by reducing state restriction.

The paradox persists when the failure to apply the LRA doctrine appropriately may produce exactly the same result as applying it by rote and rule. If LRA is not operating in a given situation, neither the state nor professionals may have an incentive to broaden the range of services to be made available to individuals. For example, the state for a variety of reasons, such as tradition, inertia, or political considerations, may choose to offer habilitation services only in institutional settings. An individual who needs habilitation in that situation has a "take it or leave it" range of "choices" as described above.

This problem is increasingly apparent. While few states, if any, have chosen to provide *no* habilitation services outside of institutional settings, many states, if not most, continue to offer the large residential facility as the mainstay of the spectrum of out-of-home living arrangements. In almost no state is there a sufficient supply of adequate community-based programs to meet the needs of those retarded citizens who need habilitation but do not require institutionalization. Where vigorous periodic review of institutionalized people has been made a reality, it is apparent that many of the residents of institutions could thrive and develop in "less restrictive placements" (those that are more nearly "normal") *if* such placements were made available. For these individuals, the lack of available alternatives puts them in the "take it or leave it" category, even though the state has set up some (but not enough) community programs.

If both LRA and its absence can work to reduce the range of individual choices available, how is this dilemma to be resolved? The potential limiting effects of LRA can be reduced and the doctrine can serve its freedom-enhancing function if it is properly interpreted and implemented. If LRA is viewed as a principle instead of a rule, i.e., a tool, it can become a means for making sure that each individual has choices available that restrict his or her freedom to the minimum extent necessary. Thus, individual choice will not be unduly impaired. The state can continue to (or can begin to) offer a range of services so long as a lack of available services does not force an individual into services more restrictive than he or she desires or needs. This is not to say that LRA can never be used appropriately to eliminate a particular "choice." Certain means of service delivery or settings can be so restrictive of liberty and so damaging to individuals that their continued existence is not justified. *But the focus of LRA implementation must remain on the creation of less restrictive alternatives, rather than on the reduction of unduly restrictive choices. In this way unnecessary restriction of human freedom can be eliminated while freedom of choice is augmented.*

This raises a very difficult question. May a retarded person or his substitute decisionmaker select an alternative which for most people would be considered "more" restrictive and, if so, under what conditions? Posing the question in this manner implies that alternatives are either more or less restrictive than one another. As we have suggested, that view of restriction may be oversimplified. But to start from the premise that it can be determined which of two alternatives is intrinsically the more restrictive still leaves us to face a difficult question of possible limitations on individual freedom of choice. As an example, the Surgeon General's finding that smoking is a hazard to health (restricts life-span) has not led to excluding smoking from the range of choices open to ordinary citizens. A potentially compounding dimension is added when it is recognized that what is the *more* restrictive alternative for one person may be the *less* so for another.

Certain proponents of LRA have advocated a literal and strict construction of the LRA principle: they contend that only the alternative rank ordered as the least restrictive should be available to the client in any given situation. This approach may reduce the amount of restriction in one dimension in our society, but it might do so at the cost of greatly reducing or eliminating free choice and self-determination and hence increasing restriction in another dimension. It also could work to limit the variety of services available and thus reduce the opportunity for experimentation with new approaches to habilitation. In our view, the rigidity of this approach makes it unattractive.

An opposite view supports an absolute affirmation of freedom of choice and contends that a retarded person or his representative is completely free to choose any alternative, regardless of the restrictions it places on the client and regardless of the fact that the client's needs can be met by less drastic means. This approach has the advantage of reducing interference with the consent process. But it has serious costs.

One problem arises when the decision-maker is the retarded client. It is difficult to ask the client to choose between two alternatives, one restrictive but familiar and the other less restrictive but also less familiar. While some clients can make such decisions, there is cause for concern about the legitimacy of this consent. Taking the decision away from the client and giving it to someone else is one way to deal with this problem. Another is to provide the client with counseling assistance. There also may be occasions in which another response would be desirable.

A different but equally serious problem arises if absolutely free choice is left to a substitute decision-maker. Substitute consent, the *Consent Handbook* points out, is a legitimate and valuable tool. Yet there is reason for greater caution when one person is deciding for another rather than for himself. Questions of restriction may raise subtle issues of conflict of interest or coercion. It may be necessary, in some cases, to devise alternatives to the usual pattern of substitute consent.

An intermediate position permits an individual the possibility of choosing an alternative regarded by some as "more restrictive." This position involves less than total limitation on freedom of choice. In our view there should be a strong presumption in favor of individual choice. But where it is shown that a particular decision, or the decision about a particular alternative, carries with it the danger of unnecessary restriction that may not be fully appreciated by a retarded person or his or her surrogate and that is not in the best interests of the retarded person, LRA may be the appropriate means to protect the retarded person from that danger even though it limits the surrogate's choice. Three recent cases illustrate the complexity and difficulty of arriving at a satisfactory role for limiting freedom of choice.

The first case is the *Pennhurst* right-to-habilitation case.[36] In this case a federal district judge concluded that the Pennhurst facility was inherently harmful to its retarded residents; no meaningful habilitation could take place there. The court ordered an end to admissions to the facility, community placements be found for existing residents, and the facility itself essentially be dismantled. It seems likely that this result will be beneficial for a considerable number of Pennhurst residents, but that is not the focus of this discussion. One effect of the court's order will be to deny to any retarded person in the Pennhurst service area the option of obtaining habilitation services in an institutional setting. Thus the court used LRA to limit the range of available choices, even though this was not the court's main purpose. Mental retardation professionals might disagree with one another over whether this type of result was compensated for by the attempt to reduce the harm that courts find often befalls institutional residents. It is important to recognize that this decision reduces the range of available choices and, hopefully, the reduction in options favorably balances the harm which that option could do against the benefit it might provide to individual clients.

The second case is *Superintendent of Belchertown v. Saikewicz.*[37] The case involved a sixty-seven-year-old profoundly retarded man who had a fatal form of cancer. The issue was whether consent could be withheld on his behalf for treatment which would produce serious side effects, be painful, require the patient to be physically restrained, and offer only a 30 to 50 percent chance of remission lasting from two to thirteen months. The testimony indicated that the cancer, if untreated, would cause the patient a painless death within a relatively short period of time. The Supreme Judicial Court of Massachusetts concluded that, although the patient himself was not competent to give or withhold consent, the decision could be made on his behalf by a court upon recommendation of a guardian *ad litem*. In support of this holding, the court found that neither the value of the patient's life nor his right to free choice were diminished by his mental disability. First, this meant that a substitute decision-maker could not withhold consent to treatment on the grounds that Mr. Saikewicz's life was of less value or less worthy of preservation than the life of a mentally normal person. Secondly, Mr. Saikewicz had the right to have another person make the decision for him on the basis of what

Mr. Saikewicz, taking into account that he is retarded, would have decided for himself had he been capable of making his own decision. The court concluded that the lower court had correctly decided that the patient would have refused the treatment had he been able to evaluate all of the facts involved in the decision.

There are many fascinating aspects to this case, but two command attention in this discussion. The first is that the court implicitly decided that this case presented factors that required a court to make the decision, rather than a guardian or family member. This means that there was something about the nature of the decision (clearly one of the options would shorten the individual's life) that made ordinary consent procedures inadequate and inappropriate. Thus the court found the nature of the potential restriction on the patient (the possibility of earlier death) sufficient to place limits on the ordinary process of choice.

The second important aspect is that while the court found the potential restriction sufficient to limit the *process* of choice, it was willing to affirm the substance of the decision, which was to opt for the categorically more restrictive alternative (or at least the alternative which was arguably more restrictive). Thus the *Saikewicz* case suggests that there is something in LRA that may be used to restrict the ordinary method of choice. It is permissible, upon an appropriate factual finding, to opt for alternatives usually regarded as more restrictive where that option is likely to have been the wish of the patient because he viewed it less restrictive. Thus the substance of the decision was not bound by an *irrebuttable* presumption that the alternative usually rank ordered as less restrictive was the preferable ˅ alternative in every case.

The third case is the celebrated *Phillip B*.[38] That case also involved a mentally retarded person whose possible life-prolonging medical treatment was at issue. The patient was a twelve-year-old boy with Down's syndrome who had a correctable congenital heart defect, which, if uncorrected by surgery, would shorten his life. The boy's parents, who had placed him in a private institution shortly after his birth, chose to withhold their consent to the corrective surgery. If successful, the surgery would be expected to lengthen his life but was not without risk. Their decision was challenged in court by the State Attorney General on the ground that they were not acting in the boy's interest. At the trial the parents stated that they refused consent because they thought it would not be in their son's best interest to outlive them, affirming that, "It would be better that he were dead than alive." The Court of Appeal upheld their decision, but did so in an opinion which did not discuss the most difficult and troubling aspects of the case. The court simply concluded that, since the operation carried significant risks, the parents' judgment should be sustained.

The relevant issue in *Phillip B.* is whether the parents were adequate substitute decision-makers for a decision involving such drastic (or restrictive) consequences since it was evident that they had concluded that their son's life had insufficient value to warrant its continuation. Whatever the ultimate result, the editors' view of LRA and of consent suggests that the court at least should have considered whether there was anything about the drastic decision to be made and the potential conflict of interest between this child and his parents that required either a different substitute decision-maker for this decision or closer scrutiny of the parents' decision by an impartial body. The *Phillip B.* case differs from *Saikewicz* in at least two important respects. While the more restrictive alternative was chosen and approved in each case, *Saikewicz* required that the decision be made by a court, while *Phillip B.* did not. And the Massachusetts court made clear that the decision could not be based upon a view that the lives of retarded people (or presumably the liberty of retarded people) were less valuable than those of the rest of the population, while, arguably, the California court implicitly approved an opposite view.

In conclusion, it should be apparent that tremendous conceptual and policy difficulties exist in the intersection between LRA and consent. Both legal doctrines have as their origin and purpose the promotion of human freedom. But their implementation may place them in conflict with one another, in which event easy answers may produce bad results. Doctrinaire adherence to one principle over the other ignores the subtleties of protecting human freedom and may work a serious disservice in the lives of retarded people.

CHAPTER III

LRA IN STATUTES

The United States Supreme Court has alluded to the LRA principle in two mental health cases but has given little substantive guidance as to the proper role of the doctrine in constitutional cases involving mentally retarded people. Lower courts probably will continue to use the doctrine as a means of reducing unnecessary restriction on the liberty of retarded people. Even if it were decided that LRA had no constitutional role, the principle would remain an important part of the legal rights of retarded people. This is because the Congress and many state legislatures have made LRA an integral part of many statutes.

Many situations are not directly governed by constitutional principles because the provisions of the Fourteenth Amendment only limit the actions of state governments. A large and rather mystifying body of case law is attempting to sort out the kinds of behavior properly attributable to the state (for example, is there "state action" if a private hospital receives governmental funds through various governmental programs?). That area of the law is currently in a state of flux. Yet where LRA as a constitutional principle does not reach a certain activity, existing statutes that incorporate LRA may make the doctrine relevant and binding.

The statutes are numerous and varied. An increasing number of states employ LRA as a component of their involuntary commitment statutes.[39] Thus advocates for persons proposed for commitment can challenge a proposed placement on the grounds that an equally acceptable alternative will require less restriction of the individual's liberty. Certain states require that the proposed placement be consistent with the client's habilitation needs or that the proposed placement be the best available alternative to meet the client's needs as well as requiring that the place of habilitation satisfy the LRA principle. Coupling LRA with a recognition of treatment needs is an important and valuable approach. It emphasizes that the proper placement is the least restrictive *among those which would adequately serve the client*. If LRA were always approached in this manner, many concerns about implementing the doctrine would be alleviated since it then would be possible to rule out "less restrictive" settings that cannot meet a client's particular needs for services.

The practical importance of LRA in commitment statutes is limited because only a small number of the retarded people in residential facilities are court committed. But where there is a working system of evaluating clients on admission in an impartial setting, i.e., a court or a quasi-judicial forum, LRA has the potential to change those proceedings from empty ritual into a dynamic exploration of how to serve the client's needs. Similarly, where periodic review of the client's needs for services (whether residential or nonresidential) is provided in a meaningful forum, LRA can serve the same functions of individualization of treatment decisions and accountability of service providers.[40]

Other state statutes that have extended LRA rights to persons receiving state services encompass a larger group of clients, at least in theory. These are the statutes which make LRA a part of a "bill of rights" or a statement of the statutory right to treatment of all clients.[41] While these statutes nominally extend the LRA principle to more clients than the commitment statutes, interpreting and enforcing rights may be more difficult. Periodic review statutes provide an automatic forum for considering how appropriate are the services a person receives, but a generally stated right often relies upon the initiative of the client to bring a possible violation to someone's attention. The editors know of no study that indicates how effective LRA and other statutory rights are when enforcement is left to client initiative. Anecdotal experience suggests that, at least in some jurisdictions, the mere enactment of a high-sounding statute may have little impact on clients' lives.[42]

States have used LRA in areas other than residential services. For one thing, they have used the principle as the basis for limited-purpose guardianship statutes.[43] LRA theory is fully compatible with such statutes because they are based upon the presumption that courts, in appointing guardians, should take no more power away from the ward than the ward's disabilities require.

State and federal legislation now requires education of handicapped children, including mentally retarded children, in the least restrictive setting, not separating them from non-handicapped children unless, even with the use of supplementary aids and resources, they are unable to learn successfully in an integrated setting.[44] The use of LRA in these statutes requires modification of what we traditionally think of as "restriction," since special classes may place no greater limitation on the physical freedom of children than do integrated classrooms. But with this modification, LRA operates much the same way in education that it operates in other areas.

Finally, state statutes have used LRA as a method of guiding treatment decisions for mentally handicapped people. Certain statutes require a finding that certain posited less drastic alternatives be shown to be ineffective before intrusive or hazardous forms of treatment can be employed. Examples of treatments limited by some states include electroshock and aversive conditioning. In at least one state, the interpretation of the law is that sterilization can be performed without the consent of a retarded person only if it is shown that all other forms of contraception (presumably less restrictive) have been tried and found unsatisfactory.[45]

Clearly, all of these statutes rest on the rebuttable presumption of treating a mentally retarded person as though he or she were not handicapped to the extent that it is appropriate to do so. They also rest on the premise that integration, even-handedness, and normalization are desirable values in dealing with mentally retarded and non-handicapped persons. For the mentally retarded person and those responsible for him, the task is to devise individually appropriate treatment, placement, education, and guardianship in light of the presumption that "normal" treatment, placement, education, and freedom from guardianship are usually the more beneficial choices in each of those cases. Not surprisingly, statutory LRA provisions carry the same possibilities of benefit and risks of harm as do the constitutional cases.

One final observation is in order about statutory LRA and the available range of choices open to retarded people. When a legislature says that retarded people have a right to receive services that involve as little restriction as possible, it is politically different from a court saying the same thing. A court that uses LRA and announces clients' rights under the doctrine does not have the resources to create alternative services. Courts have ordered states to spend money to enforce these rights, but the validity of these orders has never been conclusively settled. On its own, a court—particularly a federal court—does not have the ability to "put its money where its mouth is." This is not true, however, when legislatures enact LRA into statutes. What happens when a state legislature says all clients have a right to services consistent with LRA but then refuses to fund the creation of such services? It will prove difficult to get a court to say that, since the legislature adopted the LRA principle, it was legally obligated to create the services to turn the principle into reality. Without enforcement, LRA cannot expand the range of available choices open to retarded people. Political action may be the only resort. Legislators should not receive rewards for enacting fine sounding protections of "rights" if they are empty promises. As the old saying goes, "talk is cheap." Statutory LRA provisions will only be effective when they can operate in a service delivery system that provides an adequate range of choices for diverse individual needs.

CHAPTER IV

APPLICATIONS OF LRA TO THE LIVES OF PEOPLE WHO ARE RETARDED AND TO CURRENT PHILOSOPHIES OF SOCIAL RESPONSIBILITY TO HANDICAPPED INDIVIDUALS

The preceding chapters have demonstrated that basic constitutional principles may take on new colors when reinterpreted in the light of changing social issues. "Least restrictive" has taken on new meanings in the legal context in the past twenty years. Because some of these meanings have had an impact on service providers, the idea of "least restriction" has leaked into the lingo, where it has acquired new connotations probably not intended by the lawyers who brought it into the vocabulary of the human service professionals.

Perhaps the greatest problem faced by professionals in adopting the principle has been the tendency to invoke stereotypic responses around "mainstreaming" and "deinstitutionalization" as being, in themselves, mandatory and desirable for every individual. It is therefore useful to note that such a respected jurist as Benjamin Cardozo recognized that liberty is not defined in the abstract. He observed that restrictions which from one point of view seem more than "least" will, from another point of view, be not only justified but necessary to establish equality, and with it "true freedom." Writing more than fifty years ago, Cardozo noted that liberty was not defined in the Fourteenth Amendment. He further pointed out that although there were times in our history when the concept of liberty, and conversely of its constraint, was seen as something immutable, this idea began changing at the turn of the century. "Does (it) mean the same thing for successive generations? May restraints that were arbitrary yesterday be useful and rational and therefore lawful today? May restraints that are arbitrary today become useful and rational and therefore lawful tomorrow? I have no doubt that the answer to these questions must be yes."[46]

In addition to changing social contexts, there is another sense in which "least restriction" is destined to take on new meanings. As more is discovered about the nature of mankind and man's transactions and adjustments to his environment, restrictiveness may take on psychological connotations, as well. Legal concerns usually

41

reflect conflict perceived by human beings as arising among themselves, assuming that there is a correspondence between the law and man's understanding of human nature. This interface between a legal principle and its application is the subject of this section.

Professional personnel in human services are often at this interface as mediators of the relationship between LRA and those to whom it is applied. In this role of mediator, the professionals' task is enormous because they must converse in two domains—the intent of LRA and the client's individualized needs. Somehow the two have to be translated and converged into a single prescription.

A. The LRA Principle and Individual Mental Health

The least restrictive principle implicitly recognizes two important aspects of human functioning: (a) the importance of freedom of choice in sustaining life and hope in persons of any age, and (b) the special need for the experience of freedom, within certain limits, as a prerequisite for growth and development, especially in young people.

Consider freedom of choice. The ultimate benefit from providing the least restrictive alternative should lie in assuring to handicapped individuals a feeling of having greater control over their lives. This sense of control (dominance) has manifestations that have been linked to mental health and even survival.[47] Most people consider the loss of control through imprisonment a major deterrent to crime. Abatement of this sense of imprisonment is one of the chief reasons psychiatrists prefer voluntary hospitalization for mental patients. Providing or allowing individuals a sense of control, derived from having choices, must be an outcome, and, therefore, an interpretation of the LRA principle.

Consider the experience of freedom. Having choices is not the same as experiencing choices. This statement captures the complexity between the availability of the freedom of choice, experiencing liberation in its exercise and what is "best" for an individual. Experiencing real choices, i.e., choice within one's capacity, is important to child development, while offering intellectual and practical choices appropriate to the learner is the essence of education. It tends to curtail the right to fail.

Providing choices for people is not, in and of itself, an enhancing condition. A sense of dominance arises from meaningful choice. Thus choices are helpful only under certain conditions. Certain of

42

these conditions affecting individual perceptions of quantity and quality of choices under various circumstances are elaborated below.

1. *Quantity of choices.* In everyday life a number of choices are made by tradition or habit. Thus, a person seldom or never spends much time or conscious effort in deciding whether to put the right shoe or left shoe on first, whether to take the bus or car, whether to get to work at 8:00 a.m. or 8:30 a.m., or whether to cook fish before eating it. If we had to weigh each choice that we made during our day, we would be crippled with indecision. Too many choices take up too much time and space. Both the volume and importance can become stifling. Many experts on the problems of adolescence feel that the career, mate, and lifestyle options available today are multifarious and offered at such early ages that there is a detrimental effect on maturation. Having too many options can slow down the growth process, bringing about a lot of "shopping" behavior (identity searching) and a failure to commit oneself to a particular way of life or to the tasks of life. Similarly, one would predict that placing a wide array of many choices suddenly before a retarded person, as in precipitous and improperly implemented deinstitutionalization, would not be beneficial to that person's adjustment to the community.

The opposite condition—no choices whatsoever—is also detrimental to growth; the phenomenon of "learned helplessness" has been observed.[48] Serious restrictions placed on a person's choices may inhibit the development of an internal sense of control, causing the person to feel and act helpless, to be inordinately slow to learn, and to fail to thrive.

2. *Quality of choices.* Just as there may be too few or too many choices, there also may be choices too important or too trivial to be beneficial to an individual. Most non-handicapped persons face many decisions ranging in importance from which tie to wear to what career they will pursue. Making critical (especially irreversible) decisions is hard work and can be overwhelming. Making a trivial choice, one that lacks challenge, does not enhance a sense of autonomy. Yet choices that seem trivial to a highly competent and experienced person may give a new sense of mastery to a child or to a retarded adult. On the other hand, too tough a problem, particularly one involving poorly understood prospects, may seem overwhelming and hence will not enhance well being.

3. *Individualization.* It is clear from the discussion of quantity and quality of choices that each individual's needs can be unique with

respect to those two aspects. A "good" (growth promoting) choice for one person may be "bad" (oppressive) for another. Here "good" and "bad" refer to the experience of making the choice, not necessarily to the material outcome.

One further aspect that serves to make the problem even more complex is the fact that there is not a perfect correlation between the choices available to individuals and the choices they "feel" they have, i.e., those which serve to enhance their feeling of self-control. This can be interpreted as: "What is a choice for one person may be irrelevant for another." The parents who take a child to a fancy restaurant may find that he still insists on hamburger. Freedom to travel or move is highly valued by many people, yet there are also many people who live all their lives in the town where they were born. There is evidence to suggest that the critical variable in mental health is more the sense of having understandable choices and not the actual ("count them") options.

4. *The shaping of choices as determinants of behavior*. Just as there have been periods in history characterized by "repressive law,"[49] so there have been periods in the history of education characterized by strict mandates and emphasis on rote learning of the three R's. The consequence for retarded pupils often was a devastating experience of failure and futility. They perceived no way by which they could choose success. In reaction to this phenomenon, leaders in the care and education of retarded persons began advocating a special education environment that teachers managed to the point that the child was shielded from experiencing failure.[50] This pendulum swing also overshot the mark with no risk of failure; a consequence is that the child loses a sense of dominance, a sense that he or she can control what happens to him or her by voluntary choice of behaviors.[51]

The current use of behavior shaping techniques follows a middle course that is compatible with the importance of experiencing choice as a means to learn as well as an end in itself. The trainee is offered choices *that are within* his or her range of competence to make. He or she *can* fail but, in fact, does so infrequently. As competence increases, the range offered widens. By reinforcing responses that society considers desirable, a person is taught that certain choices are more likely than converse choices to bring him or her pleasurable consequences. The prescriptive selection of reinforcers is part of our recognition that preferences may be idiosyncratic and that the range of choice made available can be optimized differently for different

44

people at different times. It is not enough to ask: "What would I like if I were in that situation?" One must ask how a person perceives his or her situation; what is less restrictive for him or her. This idea may be represented schematically. (See Table 2.)

One implication of LRA is the need to respect these optimal ranges for each person and to assure that each range is not narrowed except for a valid social purpose.

B. The Rule of the Treatment Professional with Respect to LRA

Given the psychological complexities inherent in LRA, the individualization of the need and tolerance of choices, and the number of variables that have to be taken into account, the human services professional is in a critical position in mediating between the principle and the person.

The professional person has a different perspective from the attorney in looking at LRA. Consider the case of a client who, either by himself or through an advocate or guardian, voluntarily seeks professional aid and advice. Overt coercion is presumed absent in a "normal" professional relationship. The professional is under a number of constraints—ethical, professional, legal, and societal. All of these dictate, often contradictorily, what action should be taken for a client. Especially in working with handicapped persons, the professional is likely to be employed by an agency, rather than directly by the client. This complicates issues of loyalty and "interests." Although legal considerations have many implications for professional practice, equally important constraints on the professional stem from professional rules of ethics. These rules stipulate that the best interests of the client should be the foremost consideration. They also mandate respect for the client's individuality and autonomy. There can be a conflict between these dual goals, since the client does not always prefer what the professional views as in his best interest. Moreover, the professional has many clients, whose interests may conflict with another's.

The professional becomes an engineer of restrictiveness or freedom, a person whose role is to work with the client to come to an agreement concerning an environment which matches as closely as possible the amount of freedom that that client needs for growth and mental health. The responsibility of the professional is to manifest a sensitivity to the client's capacity to understand information. That is, transactions to which the client is an active party must take place

45

at a level comprehensible to the client. This requirement applies not only to the client's cognitive competence but also to the kinds of past experiences he or she has. There may be consent problems in getting a client to choose to move to a small group home from an institution if the client has never had the experience of living in the proposed situation. The client may gain a better environment, but the decision may not be a real choice.

TABLE 2

Schematic Representation of Range of Satisfying Choices for Persons of Differing Capacities.

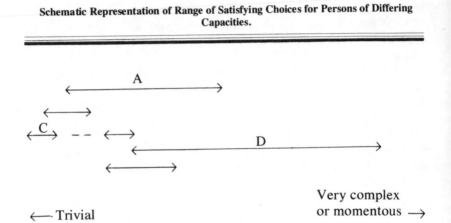

A. Albert is a typical adult.
B. Betty is a six-year-old child.
C. Carl is a profoundly retarded adult.
D. Dorothy is a genius.
E. Ellen is a moderately retarded young adult.

Schematically, when various individuals are presented with choices to the left of their optimal range, i.e., trivial choices, they are bored and do not experience satisfaction or growth. When confronted with choices which are exceptionally difficult for them, beyond their range of competence (to right) they lose "dominance" and experience frustration and even fear, and risk actual failure.

All these observations must be interpreted in the light of the basic factor that differentiates the mentally retarded person from other citizens. The retarded person is intrinsically limited, to a greater or lesser extent, in the ability to make choices on his or her own behalf, particularly where evaluating future consequences is important. The range of choices from which he or she derives that necessary sense of control, that self-esteem that psychologists say is so important, covers a different stretch of the spectrum than does the range that a college graduate might find challenging. Like the rest of us, retarded people need opportunities to succeed by their own effort and choice. These opportunities are not real unless there is also a chance to fail and perhaps an occasional experience of failure. (Can there be a sense of control if the environment is programmed to deliver M&Ms 100 percent of the time?) But these must be prescriptively tempered lest excessive failure itself become disabling and restrictive. The professional, then, engineers the choices available to the mentally retarded person, taking into account all of these variables in his or her own behavior and in the client's behavior (and perhaps in the family's as well).

What might appear to be the least restrictive environment is not invariably the most enhancing one for an individual. In many cases, present restriction may be a prerequisite to future freedom. This is the premise of compulsory schooling. In the case of a handicapped client, the extent of the client's disability, the conditions that may promote personal growth (mental health), and the anticipated impact of a given environment must be taken into account in counseling. In the case of the girl in Example 3 discussed in the introduction, the restrictiveness of the sterilization operation (permanent incapacity to procreate) must be measured against the restrictiveness imposed by birth control devices, by limitation of access to men, which may be imposed as the alternative, or by the demands of monthly menstrual periods if seen as burdensome. For non-handicapped women the weights assigned to each restriction may make the equation come out quite differently from calculating the solutions appropriate for certain retarded women.

The editors readily acknowledge that the idea of short term restriction in the name of long term independence has been used to justify and rationalize unacceptable practices in the past. These abuses must be guarded against. But the concept of trade-offs remains valid.

Weighing short and long term restrictions should lead the professional to a prognostic evaluation, i.e., the probable outcome of any particular therapy or intervention in a given environment. Will it lead toward greater independence or sense of dominance or both? To put the matter another way, if the weight of professional expertise is used to influence the client's decision toward a particular treatment, there must be a significant presumption that the client's ultimate independence, sense of dominance, increased control over his environment, or both will more than compensate for the intrusion or temporary limitation on his or her freedom. This consideration requires the professional to design a program of habilitation that looks beyond the immediate situation and a reasonable distance into the future, taking into account not only the effect of the ongoing intervention strategy but also the development status of the individual and the demand characteristics of the future environments.

The most "normal" environment is not always the least restrictive environment for a person who differs markedly from the norm. A 10-year-old mathematical genius can find the fifth grade very restrictive. It is easy but premature to base decisions of "less restrictive" on physical or nominal similarity to the norm. Too often, restrictiveness is defined as a unidimensional concept such as "size of unit." The larger the living unit, the more restrictive the environment is presumed to be. If restrictiveness is conceived of as limits on choice, the reverse may sometimes be the case. Thus, in certain family situations a retarded individual may never leave the house, never see other people, and never engage in sports or games. By contrast, in another environment he or she may have many choices of friends, of things to do, and places to go. By the same token, non-handicapped students may trade off the advantages of a large university over a small college. This example of choice of residential setting should not be construed as a promotion of large institutions; it is cited to point out that restrictiveness of a setting is not in any simple way related to the size or character of the setting. A more fine-grained analysis of both the setting and the client's role in that setting is required before its restrictiveness for him or her can be ascertained. The professional, in the unique one-to-one relationship with the client, is in a crucial position to influence that determination.

With the foregoing analyses and caveats associated with the professional-client relationship in mind, consider more specific professional activities and services.

C. Counseling and Case Management

Professionals are charged with recommending intervention by designating treatment modalities or placements. If acceptable alternatives are at hand, the professional-client relationship itself can become an opportunity for the least restrictive principle to operate. Since the concept of least restrictive alternative basically refers to the choices open to the client in any given situation, the professional counseling relationship should be exemplary of other client-caretaker-environment arrangements. The least restrictive counseling situation is one in which (a) the client is made to feel that he or she has a role in determining what happens to him or her and (b) the available alternatives impose only reasonable constraints that are understood and agreed to by the client voluntarily in the expectation of anticipated benefits—benefits that may have to be described or even demonstrated to him or her.

One of the most positive aspects of the Individual Habilitation Plan (IHP) model from the point of view of LRA is the emphasis on individual prescription. The IHP fine structures programming in a way which should be more liberating than former methods of group classification, e.g., assignment to a "trainable class" or a "non-am cottage" without individualized objectives.

The current rules for developing individual program plans (IHP, IEP) require the "participation" of the client or the clients' representative. This is an attempt to assure the individual a voice in making choices. Whether the client perceives participation as a real opportunity to influence his or her own life is a question that will be answered by formal compliance with notice and hearing procedures and more by the nuances of interaction between the professional team members, on the one hand and the client and parents on the other. This is an excellent example of the role of *felt* choice and the role of the professional (beyond the reach of law) in enhancing the client's sense of having a degree of control over what happens.

Conversely, the IHP could become a tool for restriction by (a) imposing a regimen on the client to which he or she is required to conform in the interests of those whose success is measured by achievement of predetermined goals and (b) institutionalizing the periodicity of review in a way which gives the client a sense of being trapped until the next review date.

D. The Schools

Although the LRA principle is conceptually simple, its implementation in the public school system is incredibly complex. In fact, the LRA principle runs *counter* to the *basic structure* of the public education system. Whereas the LRA principle requires focus on the individual child, public education, despite its rhetoric, is not structured in a manner to respond effectively to such a focus, particularly on a wide-spread basis. Compliance with P.L. 94-142 by providing the most enhancing environments for children with special needs calls for behaviors by school personnel that are difficult to effect, for they fly in the face of the school's perception of its own purposes as well as its historic practices.

To try to implement LRA in schools as a concept alien to the school itself is counter-productive. The effect of tinkering with only parts of the system while leaving the larger system untouched may well simply reinforce the larger, more dominant value system. Relatively few teachers involved in implementation will work upstream and in isolation to try to bring about the changes in attitude essential to implementation of least restrictive alternatives.

A larger set of attitudinal changes must be fostered so that LRA efforts can be pursued in a hospitable climate. These changes would include pursuit of the following:

1. The principle of maximum choice for all youngsters;
2. Emphasis programmatically on effective equality of educational experiences for all youngsters; and
3. Placement of the locus of programmatic decisionmaking at the point closest to implementation.

Within this context, the principle of enhancement may be pursued aggressively for children with special educational needs. Fashioning programs for developing children can be realized when the designers and implementers believe it to be a worth-while endeavor.

E. The Medical Setting

Although residential placements and special education decisions have come in for the most attention lately, the LRA principle can be invoked in almost any service context. For example, in the medical field, one may ask whether, when the patient's behavior is unacceptable and incompatible with his or her own well-being, chemotherapy is more or less "restrictive" than behavior modification. There is no universal rule. Circumstances will alter judgments. In certain medication situations only the patient, guardian, and doctor are involved, and the patient goes on about all other activities in a normal manner. In operant procedures, however, an entire group may be forced to behave in a manner controlled by the operator, e.g., the hyperactive child in a token economy system. In another situation, e.g., severe self-abuse, medication may produce a chemical "strait jacket" while aversive shock procedures eventually may allow the patient long periods of inter-shock normality.

It would appear that the procedure that allows the greatest period of time available for normative social interaction could be regarded as "least restrictive" and thus usually should govern the ethical choice of treatment of LRA. This rule-of-thumb must, of course, be weighed against severity of treatment.

Ambiguities regarding validity of consent, whether given by a retarded patient or on his or her behalf, have made some surgeons reluctant to perform elective surgery on retarded persons of any age. Thus, tendon lengthening of the cerebral-palsied retarded child is sometimes denied. Open heart surgery becomes a low priority. Ventricular shunting can become a matter of estimating thickness of cortex. Oculomotor muscle surgery is considered by many to be a cosmetic luxury if the patient is mentally handicapped. All of these options are more likely to be denied to retarded patient. Yet, if the LRA ethic were applied, these procedures would be seen as opening up new worlds of normalizing activity for mentally retarded persons who need them, even more so than with the intellectually normal. Thus it would appear that the LRA ethic can be a major source of philosophic influence in encouraging elective surgery for mentally retarded patients even when "consent" rules are wrongly perceived as imposing barriers or burdens. The need is to bring a fuller understanding of the ethics of LRA to the members of the medical profession.

F. The Retarded Offender

Since LRA is a guiding concept and not an objective and quantifiable measure, its day-to-day implications will be derived from practice modified by experience, i.e., by what works. A generation of retarded people should not be subject to the testing of social theories unless there is a strong likelihood of a benefit. This may be illustrated in the field of corrections as applied to mentally retarded people.

Interestingly, some of the recently proposed recommendations for how to respond to the mentally retarded offender have had the appearance of being less restrictive than traditional methods of the criminal justice system. Yet they often had the opposite effect. Special identification of "the mentally retarded offender" has necessarily led to prolonged delay of trial and prolonged incarceration of the accused pending a finding of fitness for trial. Civil commitment as an alternative to criminal detention has resulted in lengthier periods of confinement for the retarded defendant than imprisonment. So-called special treatment facilities have sometimes equalled the worst prison conditions. Such conditions and findings have led reformers, both in the fields of criminology and mental retardation, to suggest that the best and/or least restrictive alternatives for the mentally retarded offender may well be located in a reformed and better monitored standard criminal justice system. Since intentional "restriction" is built into the penal system, there is a special paradox here. Should the retarded person have a choice to be restricted as a "normal" offender or as a person who cannot be held accountable for his or her acts and subject to different restrictions?

G. Employment

Although there has been less controversy about LRA in the field of vocational placement and employment, one could well argue that placements should take into account the options for advancement, the availability of appropriate career ladders, and supportive fringe benefits as criteria for less restriction of future prospects. No job placement can or should be guaranteed, but neither should the trainee be put in a situation where the outcome cannot be influenced by extra effort, and/or personal competence. In fact in vocational training LRA approaches must be built into earlier decisions so as to maximize later vocational options.

H. Individual Advocacy

A particularly pertinent field is that of personal advocacy. Advocacy can be focused on opening opportunities for growth in decision-making through exercise of that function within a feasible range. Here there can be opportunities for prescriptive support that neither overprotects nor undersupports, providing "dignity of risk" while limiting the prospects of destructive failure. Table 3 illustrates a range of alternatives.

TABLE 3

Types of individual advocacy according to the least restrictive alternative (or the least drastic alternative).

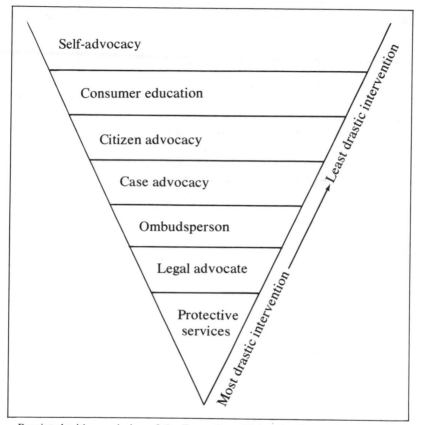

Reprinted with permission of the Texas State University Research and Training Center in Mental Retardation from "Case Advocacy: Ideology and Operation," by Barbara Jessing and Shirley Dean, in *Advocacy Systems for Persons with Developmental Disabilities: Context, Components and Resources* (Linda Baucom and Gerard Bensberg, eds.).

I. Guardianship

Within the general constructs of advocacy falls the important specific of guardianship. This ancient legal device reflects a persistent recognition that choices cannot be abrogated for any individual merely because he or she lacks the cognitive competence or the legal capacity to make them. This is one of the messages of the *Saikewicz* case mentioned earlier.

Current interest in "limited guardianship" is manifested in the recurrent concern reflected in every part of this document that "alternatives" be prescriptive. It reserves those choices that lie within the clients' spectrum of ability and thus enhance self-determination and control, both real and perceived. Guardianship is a good example of the paradox that, in order to give real options to the less competent, one must take away those that are his or hers theoretically but which cannot be exercised on his or her own initiative. A guardian has a clear duty and authority to make certain decisions, whether to choose a physician, to approve a choice of domicile or to veto a purchase "on time." The liberating effect of one-to-one advocacy for a retarded person is comparable to that of a motorized wheelchair for a paraplegic person or a telecommunication device for a deaf person.

J. Conclusion

Historically "least restrictive alternative," "equal opportunity," and "equal protection" have been concepts that had little practical effect on the lives of retarded people. Even "normalization" provides only that the normal conditions of life be made available. It is not in itself supportive of the idea that the environment should be more than normal. But the courts have recently put quite startling power into the old principles, even at the expense of the professional's own freedom. However, in the human services field creativity need not be limited by the constitution. Professionals can build on the revolution wrought by legal advocates and courts by adopting a more active principle. A good name for this new model is the "ergonomic principle."

Ergonomics is the science of the natural laws of work, more particularly, the study of human factors in design of tools, machines, and the man-made environment. By extension the term applies to all adaptations of the environment to human needs. A good architect uses ergonomic principles. Ergonomists made life in the space capsules bearable by careful attention to comfort, convenience, and efficiency under conditions of inevitable restriction.

The articulate physically handicapped are now insisting that the physical environment be adapted to accommodate their deviance from various norms, to improve their comfort and efficiency under the extraordinary natural constraints they experience. In doing so they are opposing forced segregation, but equally they are protesting forced integration. There is nothing "restrictive" about wheelchair basketball if participation is voluntary. One of the clear themes emanating from the White House Conference on the Handicapped was that "the handicapped" is an almost meaningless aggregation. The need is for categories that differentiate those who are inconvenienced by being non-ambulatory (but mobile) from those who cannot see, and in turn, those who cannot reason from those with "hidden handicaps." Handicapped individuals want the right to be different. They also want society to meet them at least half way in accommodating these differences.

The ergonomic principle subsumes LRA along with the developmental model, individuation, and affirmative action as it seeks the most enhancing, the most liberating environment that takes into account the interaction between a person's needs and abilities and the characteristics of the physical and social environment.

CHAPTER V

LRA AS A FUNCTION OF THE SERVICE SYSTEM: THE SYSTEM IS THE CONTEXT

Decisions about what constitutes the optimal or best possible treatment service for a person classified as mentally retarded are made in the context of existing human service systems and ideologies. One is rarely "free" to make service programs or individual habilitation plans in the exact manner of one's liking. Hence the frequency of such phrases as "it's another Catch 22," "the funding patterns won't allow us to do what we know is best," and "they (the clients) keep falling between the cracks." All of the individual decisions, the local decisions, are in some measure shaped by the larger systems within which they are made. In a capitalist society, for example, the rich have more choices than the poor in terms of the human services they secure for themselves. Similarly, but on a less global level, a choice of birth control methods, whether for a disabled or non-disabled family member, would certainly be influenced by forces that transcend the individual, e.g., available technologies, religious and other cultural standards, laws, cost, and accessibility. In the same vein, implementation of LRA will reflect the context in which such decisions are made.

A few examples of how the system's context can influence the application and interpretation of LRA may prove helpful here. Take, for instance, the state system that provides only one service mode to meet a particular need, e.g., a need for employment, vocational training, education, or birth control. If a state's vocational training and employment plan for severely retarded people provides the single option of a sheltered workshop, program planners, families, and retarded persons will find it exceptionally difficult to fulfill their commitment to the LRA principle. Whatever their feelings or clinical judgments about the most appropriate way to meet the LRA standard, the prevailing reality usually will render their best intentions impotent. Similarly, states that have used regional school districts to provide education for retarded children may find that this administratively efficacious service model poses a fundamental contradiction to the principle of LRA.

To the extent that service systems follow the financial structures that are predicated on political or economic considerations rather than current programmatic objectives, LRA concerns will be entangled in an unbending micro-version of economic determinism.

Two examples stand out. First, many states have developed parallel service systems with different funding sources. Psychological counselling may be offered in health, education, or social service systems, but with different means tests. Similarly, community schools receive their funding from local property taxes. They also receive some state aid for special education. In another sector of state human services, mental retardation facilities, developmental centers, regional centers, or comparable facilities also may provide educational programming for retarded students. However, in the latter instance, education may be funded entirely from the state budget. Local school districts faced with recurrent economic crises may, under the dual system circumstances, be encouraged by the 100 percent state funding to refer children into a state-operated facility. Or the local district simply may be reluctant to accept the movement of retarded children from a more restrictive state-operated facility into regular local schools. These decision makers will subordinate LRA and other programmatic considerations relevant to an individual to the more general pressures of "the system."

A second example of the economic imperative theory also involves state facilities. State residential facilities often are financed through the issuance of bonds. The bond holders must be repaid their investment and interest over twenty to thirty years. State budget officers have a self interest in maintaining the enrollments of the facilities in order to keep per capita federal and state funds flowing; these third-party payments can be used to offset the bond debt. Hence, while a state administrator of mental retardation services may desire to implement an ideology of normalization and LRA in the form of accelerating deinstitutionalization, he or she may find that his or her desire will be seen by others in state government as an economically disastrous course for newly constructed residential centers.

Thus far, editors have noted the potentially frustrating effects of single mode service systems and economic imperatives on the exercise of the LRA principle. Another potentially serious barrier to LRA is the conflict that sometimes exists between specialized separate disability-related service systems and generic service systems. Undoubtedly, implementation of LRA will have explosive repercussions as it becomes clear that many existing separate programs for disabled people, including schools for blind or deaf children, residential facilities for retarded or other handicapped people, public housing for handicapped citizens, segregated recreational programs or special purpose medical services, may violate the LRA principle. Service systems that are organized along disability lines may limit the movement of individuals from specialized services to generic ones and from one specialized service to another.

In contrast to the contextual barriers discussed above, certain service models will most certainly promote the thoughtful application of LRA. For example, certain service models will not create incentives for parallel services. Systems that create a broad range of services spanning generic and specialized services will not force more restrictive treatments. To the extent that generic systems afford extensive specialized adaptations of their generic mission and support services, guarantee equal access to the disabled, and equalize net costs to the consumer for the generic and specialized services, LRA can be implemented under non-coercive conditions.

A non-coercive atmosphere is necessary but not sufficient. Service systems must also provide the ideological climate in which LRA becomes an important, even central concern. There *also* must be a process to negotiate interpretations of LRA. The principle of normalization and the belief that services to disabled citizens are rightful, or, at least, are to be provided on a non-discriminatory basis, if adopted by service systems will set the stage for an enthusiastic pursuit of LRA. Then, if the service system incorporates processes for reviewing and consciously deciding on LRA (e.g., through individual habilitation, education, or treatment plans, peer review boards, due process procedures, citizen and systems advocacy, public awareness campaigns, external evaluations, and public planning processes), implementation surely will proceed in an effective manner.

Although P.L. 94-142, the Education for All Handicapped Children Act, explicitly promotes the concept of the least restrictive alternatives, it allows for competing forces, some more compatible with the LRA presumption and others less so. On the other hand, the law requires states to create procedures to assure that, to the maximum extent appropriate, handicapped children, including children in public or private institutions, are educated with children who are not handicapped. Yet, the law does not explicitly preclude separate schooling. Nor are state systems specifically prohibited from maintaining fiscal incentives for non-regular school placements or for dual school systems, some serving all children, disabled and non-disabled alike, and others serving only disabled children. Rather, there are established forums in which to negotiate the issue of LRA: non-discriminating evaluations, individualized education plans, impartial hearings, litigation, and state plans. In the latter two instances the legitimacy of particular financial incentives could be challenged. But at this writing, the existence of competing forces, be they funding formulas, traditional service patterns, availability of trained personnel, or others within the educational context, undoubtedly will shape the application of LRA in the states.

Analogous conditions exist in the area of residential living. The Developmental Disabilities Act and the Social Service Act (Title XX) adopt an ideology of deinstitutionalization and individual habilitation. Consistent with these aims, many state mental retardation systems, including California, Massachusetts, and Nebraska, espouse an ideology of normalization. Each of these states has adopted consumer safeguards including administrative review, individual case planning, ombudsman systems, citizens advocacy, and protection and advocacy systems. Each state has sponsored public awareness campaigns, extensive staff development programs, and research and development activities. And, in each of these states, considerable attention has been given to systems level planning for deinstitutionalization and community-based program development. To complete the analogy to education, however, it is necessary to recognize those factors that militate against an objective application of LRA. In California, the deinstitutionalization movement has partially resulted in transfers of residents from public state facilities to private nursing homes. This result has mixed blessings. Nursing home placement may be legally less restrictive but programmatically more restrictive (or at least not equally enhancing) than institutional placement, especially for people not needing traditional nursing home care. And, in all three states, budgets for community-based services have had to compete with budgets for institutional facilities. These and other states have found that the administrative process for establishing community-based residences has been more cumbersome, less responsive and, therefore, less productive than had been expected. In short, the placement of individuals into less restrictive settings has been impeded by the lack of new, adequate community-based residences, educational and vocational training, transportation, and related services.

From a systems perspective on the experiences with P.L. 94-142 and the deinstitutionalization movement, it is possible to isolate a few conditions that will facilitate the application of LRA:

1. Ideology consistent with LRA.
2. Systems-level planning to ensure available options and adoptive programming.
3. Use of generic services, including the availability of specialized support services in the context of generic settings.
4. Fiscal equity between systems so that individual case plans are developed in an uncoercive atmosphere.
5. Consumer/professional dialogue and negotiation through advocacy, periodic case review, administrative appeals, due process, ombudsman and citizen advocacy programs, etc.
6. Public awareness and professional development to expand people's understanding of and commitment to LRA.

CHAPTER VI

CONCLUSION

The LRA principle was designed to reduce unnecessary governmental restrictions in the lives of individuals. It recently has been used in constitutional litigation and adoption in statutes to perform that function in the lives of mentally retarded people. It is an appropriate and useful tool for accomplishing that task.

In certain cases of implementing LRA, however, its effect has been to reduce the range of available choices or to deny to a client those services that would best meet his needs or enhance his life. These results are both ironic and unfortunate. They are also avoidable. If LRA is interpreted and understood in the light of its original goal—enhancing personal freedom—it can be a means of increasing the alternatives available to retarded people and promoting their competence, independence, and self-sufficiency.

One way of assuring that LRA is implemented in this fashion is to remember that it is not the only consideration in choosing between service alternatives. Choices should be directed to the least restrictive alternative that will fully meet the client's present and future needs. Both needs and liberty must be weighed in the balance.

Another way of making sure LRA retains its original purpose is to recognize that restriction is not a one-dimensional concept. It is necessary to bring sophistication into determining what constitutes restriction in the lives of retarded people and in the life of each retarded individual. Oversimplification in this area can be hazardous to the well-being of retarded clients.

Finally, LRA must be implemented within a framework that values freedom of choice and provides an adequate range of nonharmful, enhancing options.

If these principles guide professionals' work, LRA will help to meet the clients' needs and protect and promote their freedom.

REFERENCE NOTES

[1]*Consent Handbook,* (H. Rutherford Turnbull, III ed. 1977).

[2]"Position Papers of the American Association on Mental Deficiency," (American Association on Mental Deficiency, 1975).

[3]*See* W. Wolfensberger, *Normalization* (National Institute of Mental Retardation, 1972).

[4]The Education for All Handicapped Children Act, Pub. L. No. 94-142, 20 U.S.C. 1412(5)(B), 1414(a)(1)(C)(iv)(1975).

[5]Meyer v. Nebraska, 262 U.S. 390, 399 (1923).

[6]*See, e.g.,* regulations at 45 C.F.R pts. 100b, 121a (1977), implementing Pub. L. No. 94-142, 20 U.S.C. § 1401, 1402, 1411-1420 (1975); regulations at 45 C.F.R. pt. 84 (1978), implementing § 504 of the Rehabilitation Act, 29 U.C.S. 794 (1973).

[7]41 Fed. Reg. 20,296 (1976).

[8]*Op. Cit., Consent Handbook.*

[9]*See, e.g.,* Covington v. Harris, 419 F.2d 617 (D.C. Cir. 1969); Halderman v. Pennhurst State School and Hospital, 446 F. Supp. 1295 (E.D. Pa. 1977); Dixon v. Weinberger, 405 F. Supp. 974 (D.D.C. 1975); Welsch v. Likins, 373 F. Supp. 487 (D. Minn. 1974), *aff'd in part, vacated in part,* 550 F.2d 1122 (8th Cir. 1977); Horacek v. Exon, 357 F. Supp. 71 (D. Neb. 1973); Wyatt v. Stickney, 325 F. Supp. 781 (M.D. Ala. 1971); 334 F. Supp. 1341 (M.D. Ala. 1971); 344 F. Supp. 373 (M.D. Ala. 1972); 344 F. Supp. 387 (M.D. Ala. 1972); *aff'd in part, rev'd in part sub nom* Wyatt v. Aderholt, 503 F.2d 1305 (5th Cir. 1974).

[10]*See* Shapiro, *Legislating the Control of Behavior Control: Autonomy and the Coercive Use of Organic Therapies,* 47 S. CAL. L. REV. 237 (1974).

[11]Not surprisingly, the minimum intrusion/LRA principle has its origins in areas far removed from the law and mentally retarded citizens. It derives originally from a case decided by the United States Supreme Court construing the commerce clause of the U.S. Constitution (U.S. CONST. art. I, § 8, cl. 3). In that case, the city of Madison, Wisconsin, attempted to prohibit the sale of milk in the city that was processed more than 25 miles outside the city. The Court struck down the city's ordinance because it found that a less drastic inspection scheme could fully serve the interests of the city in protecting its citizens from spoiled or adulterated milk without entirely preventing the sale of non-locally processed milk: *Dean Milk Co. v. Madison,* 340 U.S. 349, 354-56 (1951).

It also is used in a host of other cases requiring a balancing of individual interest with governmental needs: *Dunn v. Blumstein,* 405 U.S. 330 (1972) (right to vote); *U.S. v. Robel,* 389 U.S. 258 (1967) and *NAACP v. Button,* 371 U.S. 415 (1963) (right to associate); *Griswold v. Connecticut,* 381 U.S. 479 (1975) (right to privacy); *Aptheker v. Secretary of State,* 378 U.S. 500 (1964) and *Kent v. Dulles,* 357 U.S. 116 (1958) (right to travel); *Sherbert v. Verner,* 374 U.S. 398 (1963) (freedom of religion); and *Talley v. California,* 362 U.S. 60 (1960) (right to free speech). In all those cases, it was "state action," i.e., government activity and infringement of a constitutional right, that were the two necessary precursors or triggers for LRA. Without both, LRA cannot come into play.

[12]*See* Lessard v. Schmidt, 349 F. Supp. 1078 (E.D. Wis. 1972), *vacated and remanded on other grounds* 414 U.S. 473, *judgment modified on other grounds and reinstated* 379 F. Supp. 1376 (E.D. Wis. 1974), *vacated on other grounds and*

remanded 421 U.S. 957 (1975), *reinstated* 413 F. Supp. 1318 e.d. Wis. 1976). *See also* O'Connor v. Donaldson, 422 U.S. 563 (1975); Jackson v. Indiana, 406 U.S. 715 (1972).

[13]*See, e.g.,* Mills v. Board of Educ., 348 F. Supp. at 875.

[14]*Id.*

[15]*See, e.g.,* Parham v. J.R., 422 U.S. 584 (1979) and Sec'y v. Institutionalized Juveniles, 422 U.S. 640 (1979).

[16]Mathews v. Eldridge, 424 U.S. 319 (1976).

[17]Roe v. Wade, 410 U.S. 113 (1973); Doe v. Bolton, 410 U.S. 179 (1973); Planned Parenthood of Central Mo. v. Danforth, 428 U.S. 52 (1976); Belletti v. Baird, 443 U.S. 622 (1979).

[18]422 U.S. 563 (1975).

[19]*See, e.g.,* Royster Guano Co. v. Virginia, 253 U.S. 412, 415 (1920).

[20]*See, e.g.,* McGowan v. Maryland, 366 U.S. 420 (1961); Williamson v. Lee Optical Co., 348 U.S. 483 (1955) Frontiero v. Richardson, 411 U.S. 677 (1973); Graham v. Richardson, 403 U.S. 365 (1971); Loving v. Virginia, 388 U.S. 1 (1967).

[21]Brown v. Board, 347 U.S. 483 (1954).

[22]*See, e.g.,* Mills v. Bd. of Educ., 348 F. Supp. 866 (D.D.C. 1972); Pennsylvania Ass'n for Retarded Children v. Pennsylvania, 343 F. Supp. 279 (E.D. Pa. 1972); Maryland Ass'n for Retarded Children v. Maryland, Equity No. 100/82/77676 (Cir. Ct., Baltimore Cty., Apr. 9, 1974).

[23]LRA's linchpins are the Ninth and Tenth Amendments to the Federal Constitution. They provide, respectively, that the enumeration of certain rights in the Constitution shall not be construed to deny or disparage others retained by the people, and that the powers not delegated to the United States by the Constitution, nor prohibited by it to the states, are reserved to the states, respectively, or to the people.

These amendments assume that citizens' rights are not diluted because some of their rights are set out in the Bill of Rights and that the federal government itself is a limited government, in that it has only those powers specifically granted to it by the Constitution; accordingly, it may exercise no others, those being reserved by the states or by individual citizens.

The Ninth and Tenth Amendments set out in constitutional terms what the framers of the Constitution encapsulated in this axiom: That government governs best that governs least. The moving principle of those amendments is that the federal government should intrude only minimally into the lives of the governed.

Relying in part on the Ninth and Tenth Amendments and their principle of minimum intrusion, but more on the principle of substantive due process, the courts have attempted to balance the two familiar competing interests—a citizen's "freedom" rights against governmental intrusion, and governmental rights to act in the communal interest, notwithstanding that individual freedom is restricted thereby. Sometimes the balance is easy to strike; sometimes not. When it is the most difficult, as when the claims of the citizen seem to be as persuasive as the claims of the government, the courts have attempted to limit the amount of governmental intrusion by requiring that the scope and degree of governmental action be no greater than necessary to accomplish the government's purpose.

Substantive due process and the principles of minimum intrusion and least restriction mean that the state may act no more forcefully than is necessary to accomplish its legitimate purposes when its action may limit an individual's freedoms as guaranteed by the Federal Constitution. Thus, the principles of minimum intrusion and equal protection become techniques for accommodating the state's interests when they compete with an individual's interest.

[24]Shelton v. Tucker, 364 U.S. 479 (1960).

[25]Chambers, *Alternatives to Civil Commitment of the Mentally Ill: Practical Guides and Constitutional Imperatives*, 70 MICH. L. REV. 1108, 1150 (1972).

[26]While not the most perfect illustration of LRA as an accommodating principle, *Lake v. Cameron*, 267 F. Supp. 155 (D.D.C. 1967), certainly is one of the earliest, most oft-cited, and most persuasive. The evidence in the case was that an elderly woman did not need constant medical supervision but only attention. A nursing home or another place where there would be supervision would be adequate for her needs and out-of-hospital care (without an indication of what, if any, psychiatric care was needed) would suffice. She would wander off, was not fully conscious of time intervals, needed someone to care for her physical condition, and needed "care and kindness". But her condition did not require the complete deprivation of liberty that resulted from commitment to Saint Elizabeth's Hospital (a District of Columbia Hospital psychiatric institution) as a person "of unsound mind." The Court of Appeals for the District of Columbia held that the D.C. mental health code (providing that a court that finds a person mentally ill and because of his illness likely to injure himself may order hospitalization or any other alternative course of treatment that will be in the best interests of the person or the public) requires a trial court to inquire into "other alternative courses of treatment," including public health nursing care, community mental health and day care services, foster care, home health aide services, or private care.

What makes *Lake v. Cameron* interesting in LRA discussions is that the appeals court was not convinced that commitment was necessary and construed an existing statute to require trial courts to inquire into alternatives other than hospitalization that the person "should be required to accept." The decision nicely accommodates the respondent's interests in liberty—the more the better, based on her ability to survive in a "free" situation without harm to herself—with the state's *parens patriae* interests in protecting her in the way that is least restrictive of her liberty but still can be enforced against her will. Although the court noted that every effort should be made to find a course of treatment that the respondent "might be willing to accept," there was not even so much as a hint that state compulsion was impermissible. The only issue was: How much state compulsion is tolerable in this particular case?

Three years later, in *Covington v. Harris*, 419 F.2d 617 (D.C. Cir. 1969), the same court reaffirmed its *Lake* holding and implied that the principle of the least restrictive alternative had constitutional origins, not merely statutory ones:

> The principle of the least restrictive alternative consistent with the legitimate purposes of a commitment inheres in the very nature of civil commitment, which entails an extraordinary deprivation of liberty . . . A statute sanctioning such a dramatic curtailment of the rights of citizens must be narrowly, even grudgingly, construed in order to avoid deprivations of liberty without due process of law.

Citing *Shelton v. Tucker*, 364 U.S. 479, 488 (1960) ("even though the governmental purpose be legitimate and substantial, that purpose cannot be pursued by means that broadly stifle fundamental personal liberties when the end can be more narrowly achieved. The breadth of legislative abridgment must be viewed in the light of less drastic means for achieving the same basic purpose."), the court held that the LRA doctrine and the D.C. statute apply to intra-hospital placement as well as to whether a person may be committed to a hospital in the first place.

The D.C. cases persuaded a federal district court in Pennsylvania to hold that courts are constitutionally bound to search for less restrictive alternatives in commitment cases (*Dixon v. Attorney General*, 325 F. Supp. 966 (M.D. Pa. 1971). And in 1972, the United States Supreme Court resolved any doubts about the constitutional origins of the LRA doctrine in commitment cases in *Jackson v. Indiana*, 406 U.S. 715 (1972), concluding that Indiana's involuntary commitment statute was unconstitutional under substantive due process because it authorized the indefinite commitment of a person found to be incompetent to stand trial, saying "the nature and duration of commitment (must) bear some reasonable relation to the purpose for which the individual is committed." In *Jackson*, a mentally defective deaf mute with a mental level of a preschool child, who could not read, write, or otherwise communicate except through a limited sign language, was found incompetent to stand trial on two charges of robbery; thereafter he was committed to the state department of mental health until such time as it might certify to the court that he was sane, the commitment order being tantamount to a life sentence since the defendant was never insane and therefore could never become "sane" again so that he could be put on trial. The Court's holding was that "a person charged by a state with a criminal offense who is committed solely on account of his incapacity to proceed to trial cannot be held more than the reasonable period of time necessary to determine whether there is a substantial probability that he will attain that capacity in the foreseeable future. If it is determined that this is not the case, then the state must either institute the customary civil commitment proceeding that would be required to commit indefinitely any other citizen, or release the defendant. Furthermore, even if it is determined that the defendant probably soon will be able to stand trial, his continued commitment must be justified by progress toward that goal."

[27]*See* O'Connor v. Donaldson, 422 U.S. 563 (1975).

[28]*See, e.g.,* Covington v. Harris, 419 F.2d 617 (D.C. Cir. 1969).

[29]325 F. Supp. 781 (M.D. Ala. 1971); 334 F. Supp. 1341 (M.D. Ala. 1971); 344 F. Supp. 373 (M.D. Ala. 1972); 344 F. Supp. 387 (M.D. Ala. 1972); *aff'd in part, rev'd in part sub nom* Wyatt v. Aderholt, 503 F.2d 1305 (5th Cir. 1974). The court in *Wyatt* defined treatment as care, provided by mental health professionals and others, that is adequate and appropriate for the needs of the mentally impaired resident, including a humane physical and psychological environment. 334 F. Supp. at 1343.

[30]357 F. Supp. 752 (E.D. N.Y. 1973); *consent decree approved sub. nom.* New York State Ass'n for Retarded Children v. Carey, 393 F. Supp. 715 (E.D. N.Y. 1975).

[31]373 F. Supp. 487 (D. Minn. 1974), *aff'd in part, vacated in part,* 550 F.2d 1122 (8th Cir. 1977).

[32]446 F. Supp. 1295 (E.D. Pa. 1977), *stay denied,* 451 F. Supp. 233 (E.D. Pa. 1978), 612 F. 2d 84 (3d Cir. 1979), cert. granted, 100 S. Ct. 2984 (1980). *See also* Wuori v. Zitnay, Civ. No. 75-80-SD (D. Maine, July 14, 1978); Evans v. Washington, Civ. Act. No. 76-0293 (D.D.C. June 14, 1978).

[33]*See* Stone, *Overview: The Right to Treatment—Comment on the Law and Its Impact,* 132 AM.J. PSYCHIAT. 1125, 1132 (1975).

[34]See Coval, Gilhool, and Laski, *Rules and Tactics in Institutionalization Proceedings for Mentally Retarded Persons: The Role of the Courts in Assuring Access to*

Services in the Community, 12 EDUC. AND TRAINING OF THE MENTALLY RETARDED 177 (1977).

[35] See Harvard Law Review, *Mental Health Litigation: Implementing Institutional Reform,* 2 MENTAL DIS L. REP. 221 (1977); Lotman, *Enforcement of Judicial Decrees: Now Comes the Hard Part,* 1 MENTAL DIS. L. REP. 69 (1976); Note, *The Wyatt Case: Implementation of a Judicial Decree Ordering Institutional Change,* 84 YALE L. J. 1338 (1975).

[36] *Supra,* note 32.

[37] 77 Mass. Adv. Sh. 2461, 370 N.E. 2d 417 (1977). Despite its nearly unique facts, *Saikewicz* is pecularily LRA-related. To be sure, the Court held that acknowledged state interests that would cause certain types of restriction (physical restriction and treatment-related pain and disorientation) were insufficient to overcome the choice to refuse treatment; a mentally retarded person and his representatives have the same right as others to choose a very restrictive outcome (death more quickly than if treatment were accepted). But it reached this result in a case that involved the treatment, care, and life of only one person, not many. This is the important distinction between *Saikewicz* and *Pennhurst*.

Arguably, the *Saikewicz* principle should be and, by proper legal interpretation, is limited to the facts in the case, but inevitably someone will attempt to stretch the principle to apply to similar but not identical situations. For example, is a mentally retarded person entitled to choose one therapy or placement over another, including a more "restrictive" or "intrusive" one in preference to a less restrictive or intrusive one? Is the principle of choice, not a notion of restrictiveness (death, after all, is both highly restrictive and highly liberating), a more highly valued principle than "less restriction" (when "less restriction" implies a duty of the state to treat and the inability of the retarded person legally to resist that treatment)? Is the principle of "subjectivity" in decisions more highly valued than one of "objectivity" (based on a "reasonable man" doctrine)?

It is tempting to conclude that the answers to these questions are invariably "yes," but such answers must remain highly tentative in light of the court's finding that two of the four relevant state interests were inapplicable, another was satisfied by the facts of the case, and a final one was properly balanced in this case in favor of individual privacy and choice, not state concerns for preserving life. If the state interests had not been as fully satisfied, would the same result have been obtained? That is surely arguable especially in light of state interests that come into play in other cases.

Saikewicz nevertheless is indispensable to an analysis of LRA because it establishes boundaries for individual choice beyond which the state may not intrude, articulates principles of individual choice (as determined on a subjective basis) as belonging to a retarded persons and his representatives, justifies (on the principle of choice) a type of restriction (death) that many "reasonable" people would conclude is intolerable as long as some treatment is available, and gives comfort to arguments that "less restrictive" is to be defined in nonnormative terms.

Thus, *Saikewicz* and *Pennhurst* apparently manifest opposite concerns: the former decision emphasizes the importance of freedom of choice and the latter limits the range of individual freedom of choice (by restricting the ways in which the state may act) in order to improve the quality of treatment. Both cases are nevertheless applications of the LRA principle.

To see that this is so, it is important to deal with a second series of cases, the "Woodhaven cases," particularly *In Re: Joyce Z., a minor.* In *Joyce Z.* (discussed in *Coval* et al, *supra,* note 34), the issue was whether a profoundly retarded and seriously brain-damaged 13-year-old girl, classified as "dependent and neglected," should be committed to Western State School and Hospital, a mental retardation center in Woodhaven, Pennsylvania. Because of her condition, Joyce obviously was a bona fide candidate for placement at Western, especially in light of caseworker testimony that all other *potential* placements had been exhausted without success and commitment was "the only option left."

In the commitment hearing, however, the trial court found that the unit in which Joyce would be placed at Western would be unable to give her any treatment or habilitation, to which she was constitutionally and statutorily entitled (because the institution was so overcrowded and understaffed), and would indeed cause her harm. Accordingly, the court required the petitioners, local mental health and mental retardation professionals, to search for and find suitable foster care for her.

While the case clearly indicates that courts, upon finding institutional placement inappropriate or detrimental and appropriate alternatives not available, must in turn enter orders that create services in "the least restrictive settings" (in more appropriate, community-based settings, as in *Joyce Z.* and the other Woodhaven cases) and remove administrative, bureaucratic, and fiscal obstacles to such placements (with the result that "least restrictive" is defined not in the narrow sense of what is available but in a broader sense of what may become available), it is likewise clear that "least restrictive" is interpreted in light of the individual's needs for treatment, not solely in light of his "liberty" interests. After all, a finding that a particular placement would be detrimental and a denial of treatment rights deals in the first instance with rights to appropriate treatment and habilitation. The fact remains that commitment to custody in a foster home was ordered and that involuntary placement was the overriding characteristic of the hearing. Restrictiveness is an inherent characteristic of commitment cases.

In a case with different facts, it may be that community placement, even after all *available* and all *possible* alternatives are explored, created, and tried, would be found "detrimental" or at least not beneficial and that the only placement that would afford the retarded person a right to treatment and habilitation may be in "an institution." The placement that may have been too restrictive for Joyce (because of the characteristics of Western and Joyce) may not be as restrictive for another. There are, as well, some administrative, bureaucratic, and fiscal obstacles that may be immutable, even to court orders. That fact constitutes a type of restriction.

Joyce Z., then, in making plain the needs to evaluate the LRA principle in light of both liberty interests (as did *Saikewicz*) and treatment needs (as did *Pennhurst*), demonstrates a somewhat paradoxical balancing process by which these three cases reach results ranging from the presumptively least to the most "restrictive" application of LRA.

After reviewing the major cases raising LRA considerations in states dealing with mentally retarded people, it is safe to say that a sometimes unrecognized paradox exists in the use of the LRA doctrine: enforced placement of any kind (whether the state is exercising its *parens patriae* or police powers) is as restrictive as enforced placement of any other kind, since the common element in all cases is the enforced placement, i.e., the commitment of a person to one setting or another without his consent. Likewise, enforced treatment of one kind may be as restrictive as enforced treatment of any other kind, or even as restrictive as no treatment at all. Similarly, forced integration or "mainstreaming" may be as restrictive as forced segregation.

Given the necessity for the state sometimes to act without the consent of the affected person, the person's restriction is inherent and inescapable. His wishes, consent, and opportunity for choice are at best minimal and at worst nonexistent.

But not all state action of a restrictive type—of a type that largely if not entirely disregards the affected person's consent and choice, i.e., his "freedom"—need be as restrictive (as potentially infringing on his rights to treatment and habilitation) as another. The LRA doctrine requires professionals, courts, and others charged with the responsibility of caring for retarded people (including their families and guardians) to create the conditions, within situations where choice is clearly legally irrelevant (e.g., commitment or compulsory education), that are the most apt to enhance the ability and ameliorate the deficits of the retarded person. The understandable concern of all parties with involuntary placements, settings, and treatment modalities does not obscure this central message of the LRA doctrine—the concern with enhancement.

It is not sufficient to discuss LRA as it operates or should come into play in the "involuntary" cases of commitment and compulsory education, for these cases are by no means the majority of cases in which LRA can and should be brought to bear. There are important decisions made voluntarily by mentally retarded people, their representatives (families and guardians), and mental retardation professionals. Not every choice of placement or treatment modality or decision not to be placed or treated is "involuntary," even by the longest stretch of one's imagination.

In the "voluntary" decision, it is especially paradoxical that the LRA doctrine may be becoming a method of restriction, not a technique for accommodating the sometimes competing interests of the state and the retarded individual. For example, in the treatment/habilitation cases, there is an unmistakable tendency for the courts to require the mentally retarded person to take advantage of his rights to treatment/ habilitation. Paradoxically, this is not how courts usually deal with handicapped adults or representatives of nonhandicapped minors. Likewise, in both the treatment and placement cases, there is a trend for the courts to restrict the mentally retarded person's freedom of choice (or his representative's freedom of choice) by requiring him to go certain places or take certain treatment.

This trend is partially explainable on the ground that advocates (both legal and treatment professionals who seek certain goals through court-ordered law reform) for mentally retarded individuals presume that the mentally retarded individual wants to exercise his LRA rights—his right to be in a place or treatment program that is less restrictive of his "liberty" than another and is simultaneously conducive to his development. This presumption seems so strong and the burden of overcoming it so great that it may rise to the level of an irrebuttable presumption; at the very least, it is rebuttable only by a very strong case. With the exception of *Saikewicz,* no court has yet found that a mentally retarded person may choose a setting or treatment that is more restrictive of his liberty than another. This may be because no case has been tried in which the facts show that a presumptively more restrictive placement (such as an "institution") or more restrictive treatment (such as electroshock therapy) is more enhancing than a placement or treatment that is less confining of a person's liberty, or, perhaps more accurately, less *nonnormative* or *nonnormalizing.* It also may be so because more restrictive placements and treatments are indeed not as enhancing as less restrictive ones, but this proposition is arguable, especially when

71

alternative forms of psychological restriction have to be weighed against legal restrictions. The SIB example in the introduction is a case in point.

It is by no means an easy task to try to reconcile the highly restrictive effects of the LRA doctrine (restrictive of choice) with the *Saikewicz* principle: choice belongs to the retarded person and may be exercised by him or his representatives in ways that "reasonable" people would not condone, notwithstanding that the choice assures a more restrictive effect than other choices might. In *Saikewicz,* the court found that the state interests in preserving Saikewicz' life were insufficient to prevail against his interests in privacy and autonomy, in freedom of choice.

It is now necessary to define the state's interests so that it can be decided whether they prevail over the mentally retarded person's competing "freedom" interests in choice and autonomy.

State interests (interests that state officers, such as judges or mental retardation professionals, or the state itself may have) may include the following:

1. The state, particularly the courts, may be interested in correcting the conditions of its own "institutions" for the mentally retarded (in short, in curing itself of its own disease, of being both physician and patient) by having them reformed or closed down. The *Wyatt-Welsch-Willowbrook-Pennhurst* line of cases seems to illustrate that interest. It follows that attempts at correcting self-created (state-created) conditions will reach a large number of mentally retarded people and will (presumptively) benefit most if not all of them. Accordingly, the choice of one or a few of them to remain in insufficient conditions must be submerged to the interests of the rest to be rescued from such conditions. The principle of the greater good for the greater number is at work here.

Also implicated is another principle, which is the duty of the state to satisfy the constitutional and statutory rights of mentally retarded people to treatment and habilitation. Rights create duties, and the state's duties to all retarded persons prevail over the wishes of some retarded persons to waive their rights and forgive state noncompliance with the duties. A constitutional principle is at work here, with a result that says that constitutional rights may not be waived, even where the waiver would affirm that the mentally retarded person has equal standing with the non-handicapped (who may waive their rights in many cases) and is entitled to exercise a right—the choice to waive some rights—that may be more valuable than the rights he or she seeks to waive. Both principles result in restricting someone's right to choice. Is that result defensible?

2. The state is interested in preventing its "institutions" from reverting to the "warehouse" and "dumping grounds" that they once were. Accordingly, the state requires that residents of the institutions be discharged, the institutions dismantled, no more admissions be made to those institutions, and, concomitantly, community services be created where none now exist. The *Joyce Z.* case seems to represent this interest. As with the first state interest, this one proceeds on a greater-good/greater-number rationale as well as on a constitutional right-duty principle. Similarly it causes restrictions and raises the same question about results.

3. The state is interested in integrating retarded people with non-handicapped people. Accordingly, it must prevent institutional placement, discharge institutional residents, educate retarded people with nonretarded people to the maximum extent appropriate for the retarded students, and prevent discrimination against retarded people. Here, the apparent concern is for not only the mentally retarded person (i.e., that he or she not be excluded from an opportunity to be with non-handicapped people)

but also the non-handicapped person (i.e., that he or she "learn" from the presence of handicapped people in the "community").

Provisions against discrimination are one thing (and highly necessary). It may be, however, quite another to take the policy of antidiscrimination and transform it into a policy that compels integration. Compelling a certain result (in this discussion, integration) is a restrictive state action—it constrains the choice of people who do not want to be forced to mingle with each other. Its effect on both the non-handicapped and handicapped is similar: neither is given unlimited freedom of choice.

4. The state is interested in dismantling the restrictions that laws and mores have placed on retarded individuals. One technique toward this end is antidiscrimination legislation, and another is rights-granting legislation. Both types of legislation have their judicial counterparts: the cases have dismantled restrictions (at the risk of creating others) and granted rights. One reason that compels a state to move in these directions is that it is bad governmental policy to discriminate because of unalterable or unchosen characteristics of the person discriminated against. Such a policy says something unseemly about the government itself and about the person. Another reason is that generally it is laudable to treat all people alike, to recognize their essential sameness by resorting to principles of equity, evenhandedness, equality of opportunity (and sometimes equality of output), and egalitarianism. Equal protection under the laws is the controlling legal principle. It is superimposed on the mentally retarded person (a member of the "class" of people entitled to be treated equally with respect to each other and with respect to the non-handicapped) without regard to whether he or she chooses to be treated equally. Most would choose at least equal treatment, but some may not.

5. The state is interested in the retarded citizen's being protected from neglect, abuse, or exploitation by others, including family, guardians, and service-providers. Because the state presumes or finds that it cannot implicitly trust those people, it regulates their activities, prohibiting some types of activities, requiring others, and setting limits and conditions on still others. Distrust, which in many but not all cases is well founded, results in a restriction on all, including the retarded person.

6. Finally, the state is interested in a retarded person's liberty not simply because of the value of liberty (including the rights of choice) as a constitutional guarantee but also because of its value for developmental and enhancement purposes (see Chapter III, this document). Because more people (retarded individuals and those people charged with responsibility for them) will choose to forego their liberties (or some people's notions of liberty), it is important to circumscribe their liberty of choice so that other liberties (in placement, treatment, and education) may be more surely safeguarded.

There may be other legitimate state interests. Be that as it may, it is gainsaid that the interests discussed above can and do prevail over the freedom of choice belonging to retarded and non-retarded people (their families, guardians, and service providers). The issue is not whether the interest in freedom of choice is to be the paramount one. Rather it is when, under what circumstances, and by what procedures is it determined that these state interests prevail when they conflict with the interest in choice. The LRA doctrine, still in its infancy, threatens to seriously skew the answer to this question. The exercise of choice is, after all, the exercise of a freedom to choose both more and less restrictive placements, treatments, or whatever; it is a technique that enables. One should always be cautious about disabling an enabling technique.

[38]Bothman v. Warren B. *In Re Phillip B.*, 92 Ca. App. 3d 796, 156 Cal. Reptr. 48 (1979), cert. den. 100 S. Ct. 1597 (1980).

[39]Hoffman and Foust, *Least Restrictive Treatment of the Mentally Ill: A Doctrine in Search of its Senses,* 14 SAN DIEGO L. REV. 1100 (1977).

[40]*See, e.g.,* CAL. WELF. & INST. CODE § 4502(a) (West Cum. Supp. 1977); NEB, REV. STAT. §§ 83-1, 141-146; Sub. H.B. No. 244, 1975 Ohio Laws 2026; Act 143, 1976 Pa. Laws 817. For discussion of zoning restrictions see Chandler and Ross, *Zoning Restrictives* in THE MENTALLY RETARDED CITIZENS AND THE LAW 307 (Kindred et al. ed. 1976); 2 MENTAL DIS. L. REP. 17 (1977).

[41]*See, e.g.,* N.C. GEN. STAT. § 122-55.1 (1973). Some states limit these rights to residential clients. Others extend them to clients receiving services in the community.

[42]Pub. L. No. 94-103, 45 U.S.C. § 6001 (1975).

[43]2 MENTAL DIS. L. REP. 44 (1978); Comment, *North Carolina Guardianship Laws — The Need for Change,* 54 N.C.L. Rev. 389 (1976); N.C. GEN. STAT. ch 35 art. IA (Cum. Supp. 1977).

[44]Pub. L. No. 94-142, 20 U.S.C. §§ 1401, 1402, 1411-1420 (1975); H. TURNBULL and A. TURNBULL, FREE APPROPRIATE PUBLIC EDUCATION: LAW AND IMPLEMENTATION, ch. 6 (1978).

[45]North Carolina Ass'n for Retarded Children v. North Carolina, 420 F. Supp. 451 (E.D.N.C. 1976).

[46]Cardozo, The Nature of the Judicial Process. (New Haven, Ct.: Yale University Press, 1922 4th printing, 1978), pp. 76-77.

[47]E.J. Langer and Roding, J., "The Effects of Choice and Enhanced Personal Responsibility for the Aged. A Field Experiment in an Institutional Setting." *Journal of Personality and Social Psychology,* 1976, *34,* 191-198, and M.E.P. Seligman, *Helplessness: On Depression, Development and Death.* (San Francisco: W.H. Freeman, 1975).

[48]R.F. DeVellis, "Learned Helplessness in Institutions," *Mental Retardation,* 1977, *15*(s), 10-13.

[49]P. Nonet & P. Selznick, *Law and Society in Transition: Toward Responsive Law* (1978).

[50]E. Johnstone, "Discipline in the Teaching of Children Three Years or More Below Normal" (N.J. Dept. of Public Instructions, 1978).

[51]Cobb, *The Attitude of the Retarded Person Towards Himself, in SOCIAL WORK AND MENTAL RETARDATION (N. Schreiber ed. 1970).*

BIBLIOGRAPHY

Adamson, J., & Schmale, A. Object loss, giving up, and the onset of psychiatric disease. *Psychosomatic Medicine*, 1965, *27*, 557–576.

Adler, A. Individual psychology. In C. Murchinson (Ed.), *Psychologics of 1930*. Worcester MA: Clark University Press, 1930.

Altman, I. *The environment and social behavior*. Monterey, California: Cole Publishing Co., 1975.

Baron, R. A. Attraction toward the model and models competence as determinants of adult imitative behavior. *Journal of Personality and Social Psychology*, 1970, *14*(4), 345–351.

Bettelheim, B. Individual and mass behavior in extreme situations. *Journal of Abnormal and Social Psychology*, 1943, *38*, 417–452.

Budoff, M., & Gottlieb, J. Special-class EMR children mainstreamed: A study of an aptitude (learning potential) × treatment interaction. *American Journal of Mental Deficiency*, 1976, *81*(1), 1–11.

Chalmers, D. K., Horner, W. C., & Rosenbaum, M. E. Social agreement and the learning of matching behavior. *Journal of Abnormal and Social Psychology*, 1963, *66*, 556–561.

Corah, N., & Boffa, J. Perceived control, self-observation, and response to aversive stimulation. *Journal of Personality and Social Psychology*, 1970, *16*, 1–4.

de Charms, R. *Personal causation*. New York: Academic Press, 1968.

Dennis, W., & Dennis, M. G. Infant development under conditions of restricted practice and minimum social stimulations. *Genetic Psychology Monographs*, 1941, *23*, 147, 149–155.

Dennis, W., & Sayegh, Y. The effect of supplementary experiences upon the behavioral development of infants in institutions. *Child Development*, March 1965, *36*(1).

Dybwad, G. Action implications, U.S.A. today. In R. Kugel & W. Wolfensberger (Eds.), *Changing patterns in residential services for the mentally retarded*. Washington: President's Committee on Mental Retardation, 1969.

Ferrari, N. A. Institutionalization and attitude change in an aged population: A field study and dissidence theory. Unpublished doctoral dissertation, Western Reserve University, 1962.

Gampel, D. H., Gottlieb, J., & Harrison, R. H. A comparison of the classroom behavior of special-class EMR, integrated EMR, low IQ, and nonretarded children. *American Journal of Mental Deficiency*, 1974, *79*, 16–21.

Goffman, E. *The presentation of self in everyday life*. New York: Doubleday, Anchor Books, 1959.

Goffman, E. *Asylums*. New York: Doubleday, 1961.

Gottlieb, J., Gampel, D. H., & Budoff, M. Classroom behavior of retarded children before and after reintegration into regular classes. *Journal of Special Education*, 1975, *9*, 307–315.

Greenberg, D., Uzgiris, I. C., & Hunt, J. McV. Hastening the development of blink-response with looking. *Journal of Genetic Psychology*, 1968, *113*, 167–76.

Hall, E. T. *The hidden dimension*. New York: Doubleday, 1966.

Ittleson, W. H., Proshansky, H. M., & Rivilia, L. G. A study of bedroom use on two psychiatric wards. *Hospital and Community Psychiatry*, 1970, *21*(6), 177–180.

75

Kelvin, P. A social psychological examination of privacy. *British Journal of Social and Clinical Psychology,* 1973, *12,* 248–261.

Langer, R. J. The illusion of control. *Journal of Personality and Social Psychology,* 1975, *32,* 311–328.

Langer, E. J., & Rodin, J. The effects of choice and enhanced personal responsibility for the aged: A field experiment in an institutional setting. *Journal of Personality and Social Psychology,* 1976, *34,* 191–198.

Lawrence, E. A., & Winschel, J. F. Locus of control: Implications for special children. *Exceptional Children,* 1975, *41,* 483–490.

Lefcourt, H. M. The function of the illusions of control and freedom. *American Psychologist,* 1973, *28,* 417–425.

Litrownik, A. J., Franzini, L. R., & Turner, G. L. Acquisition of concepts by TMR children as a function of type of modeling, rule verbalization, and observer gender. *American Journal of Mental Deficiency,* 1976, *80*(6), 620–628.

McMahon, A., & Rhudick, P. Reminiscing, adaptational significance in the aged. *Archives of General Psychiatry,* 1964, *10,* 292–298.

Olson, D. R. *Cognitive development: The child's acquisition of diagonality.* New York: Academic Press, 1970.

Osmond, H. Function as the basis of psychiatric ward design. *Mental Hospitals,* 1957, *8,* 23–30.

Rapaport, A. Some perspectives on human use and organization of space. Paper presented at Australian Association of Social Anthropologists, Melbourne, Australia, May 1972.

Rodin, J., Crowding, perceived choice, and response to controllable and uncontrollable outcomes. *Journal of Experimental Social Psychology,* in press.

Rosenbaum, N. E., & Tucker, I. F. Competence of the model and the learning of imitation and non-imitation. *Journal of Experimental Psychology,* 1962, *63,* 183–190.

Schmale, A. Relationships of separation and depression to disease. I. A report on a hospital medical population. *Psychosomatic Medicine,* 1958, *20,* 259–277.

Schmale, A., & Iker, H. The psychological setting of uterine cervical cancer. *Annals of the New York Academy of Sciences,* 1966, *125,* 807–813.

Seligman, M. E. P. *Helplessness.* San Francisco: Freeman, 1975.

Stephens, M. W., & Delys, I. External control expectancies among disadvantaged children at preschool age. *Child Development,* 1973, *44,* 670–674.

Stotland, E., & Blumenthal, A. The reduction of anxiety as a result of the expectation of making a choice. *Canadian Review of Psychology,* 1964, *18,* 139–145.

Strichart, S. S., & Gottlieb, J. Imitation of retarded children by their nonretarded peers. *American Journal of Mental Deficiency,* 1975, *79*(5), 506–512.

Turiel, E. Developmental processes in the child's moral thinking. In F. H. Mussen, J. Langer, & M. Covington (Eds.), *Trends and issues in developmental psychology.* New York: Holt, Rinehart, & Winston, 1969.

White, B. L. *Human infants: Experience and psychology development.* Englewood Cliffs, N.J.: Prentice-Hall, Inc., 1971.

Wolfsenberger, W. *The principle of normalization in human services.* Toronto: National Institute on Mental Retardation, 1972.

5714